*To Carol & Rich*
*Thanks for your clues*
*Stay Resilient*
*Rus/2020*

# 30 + 1

## RESILIENT STORIES

*Michael Ballard*

*Michelle Carty*

Editorial Development

by Linsey Fischer

# Table Of Contents

Acknowledgments ......................................................................... v

Foreword ........................................................................... vii

Introduction .......................................................................... xi

**Chapter One:** How I turned Hopelessness into Hopefulness ................. 1
*Michael Ballard*

**Chapter Two:** Serene Cynthia Carty ..................................... 5
*Michelle Carty*

**Chapter Three:** Travelling Through Adversity ......................... 9
*Cheryl Zhang*

**Chapter Four:** Ashes.......................................................... 13
*Jonathan Tarrant*

**Chapter Five:** Grow Through What You Go Through ..................... 17
*Thea Cosma*

**Chapter Six:** Kreature.......................................................... 21
*Ryan Gumbert*

**Chapter Seven:** Rebuilding My Name ................................... 25
*Cleoni Crawford*

**Chapter Eight:** Keep Calm And Carry On ............................ 29
*Connie Whitmore*

**Chapter Nine:** Turn Your Pain Into Power............................... 33
*Jessica De Serre Boissonneault*

**Chapter Ten:** Anxiety, Addiction & Accountability....................... 37
*Katie McDermott*

**Chapter Eleven:** Beautifully Blended & Empowered ..................... 43
*Tina Clements*

**Chapter Twelve:** God-Given Resilience ................................. 47
*Dr. Venise Haynes*

**Chapter Thirteen:** Your Journey is Your Reward....................... 51
*Kathi Holliday*

**Chapter Fourteen:** Tearing Down My Castle ......................... 55
*Mike Popovici*

**Chapter Fifteen:** Focus on Faith ........................................ 59
*Russ Hansen*

**Chapter Sixteen:** Undercover Truth .......................................63
True Bryant

**Chapter Seventeen:** Resiliency, Embrace the Possible ..........................69
Susy Giddy

**Chapter Eighteen:** The Dream...........................................73
Darrel Howell

**Chapter Nineteen:** The First Step To A New Life...............................77
Andrew Alberlan

**Chapter Twenty:** Learning to Love Me .............................81
Jennifer Doyle

**Chapter Twenty-One:** Live4Life Now ...........................................85
Robert Lawrence

**Chapter Twenty-Two:** My Greatest Gift...............................89
Kelly (McDermott) Chiasson

**Chapter Twenty-Three:** My Treasured Gift ............................93
Theresa Cole

**Chapter Twenty-Four:** Resiliency By Law ................................97
Samantha F. Glass

**Chapter Twenty-Five:** We Are Strong Together .............................101
Satie Sekhon

**Chapter Twenty-Six:** How Resiliency Showed Me The Right Path ....105
Carl Carty

**Chapter Twenty-Seven:** Through Grief.............................109
Marcelle Wynter

**Chapter Twenty-Eight:** Resilient for My Clients .............................113
Cindy Zupanoovic

**Chapter Twenty-Nine:** Life Redesign .............................117
Rosetta Qadhi

**Chapter Thirty:** Giving Back...........................................121
Gloria Duguay

**Chapter Thirty-One:** Our First Business.............................125
Roy Cleeves

**Conclusion:**...........................................129
**Editor:** ...........................................131

# Acknowledgments

❧

Well, we did it! *30+1 Resilient Stories* is here. Despite social distancing and all the other trials and tribulations, we made it.

Thank you to Mr. Gordon So for planting the seeds to all of us to do a collaborative book together. With teamwork, we've made the dream work.

This journey that led me into my deep interest in Resilience started at the very young age of six when I had my concussion: then the chronic and acute health issues, and that workplace robbery. However, here I am, blessed to be here. A high mileage scratch and dent model yet.

I never once thought it would turn into a career. Yet, it did. **Resiliency for Life** was born in the late 1980s. It allowed me to travel from Bermuda to Singapore, Halifax to Victoria to New Orleans, and many points in between. All the while, I was working with firms such as Alberta Health, Bell, IBM, CMA Ontario, CanGrands, CPSA, Ontario Nursing Home Assoc., and hundreds of other clients. Now I am very pleased to have a co-authored book with *30+1* stories of Resilience.

Thank you to Michelle for introducing us to so many interesting people who became authors and helping us make this happen. Thank you to our Editor, Linsey, for putting these pages together and working with our authors to ensure each story flowed. To Samantha and Kelly for all of their efforts in the background and online! Wow, all the energy. Last and not least, the co-authors for your participation to bring the book together.

The purpose of my work and this book is to share powerful stories. When we have the courage to shine a light on our challenges and some of the worst times in our lives, we can help others through sharing the lessons learned, the comebacks, and triumphs so people can discover that they are not alone. Hope is a very powerful gift to share through stories of sadness and triumph.

I trust you enjoy this book as much as I have. The 30+1 title is significant as for those that are struggling; I ask you to hang on for just one more day +1. I am certain you'll enjoy these insightful stories of bravery and courage—upsets and downturns, yet ultimately triumphs.

*Michael H Ballard*

# Foreword

What is resiliency? What does it mean to lead a resilient life? What you will read on these pages are people's testaments to resiliency. You will read stories of battles fought and won, challenges overcome, and consistent and deliberate intentions to bounce back, to get up one more time than they fell.

These stories will illustrate that the cork will always float to the top. The cork is always buoyant, and so are we. The human body is made up of more than half water, after all. I've learned that the more we can surrender to what is before us, the better we can deal with changing tides. I have learned to change the questions I ask myself from, "why is this happening to me" to "what can I learn from this?"

In 2018 I was diagnosed with Hodgkin's lymphoma. The oncologists and doctors told me early that my attitude would be the most important part of my healing and to start with the end in mind. So, as I embarked on what would be about a year of intense chemotherapy, I was focused on the finish line. In my mind, this wouldn't be a fight with cancer, but instead, a path to getting healthy.

During treatments, when my body was breaking down and rebuilding itself, I was faced with what seemed like almost insurmountable challenges. At the time, I thought it could not have been worse timing—a looming election in which I was about to bid for my third term as mayor was upon us, and I was sick. Really sick. Many days I sat and looked out the window, not reading, not watching TV, just staring outside. At times, this was all I had the energy to do. For a person like me who had run several businesses, chaired boards, was an active person, healthy, fit, very involved in my three kids' lives, and had run a major tourist city for the last eight years, sitting still was foreign.

The challenges I faced in the months ahead, like many cancer patients do, included: significant weight loss, lesions on my body, loss of hair, debilitating exhaustion, and insomnia, just to name a few. In addition, I was engrossed in the internal challenge of what to do with the election. I knew that putting my name into the ring would have to mean surrendering completely— surrendering running a campaign to my team-members, close friends, and family. Surrendering to the voters, hoping that they would appreciate my leadership thus far and elect me for another term, based solely on past record. Surrendering to the direction this disease was taking my life, and focusing on the next stage of healing, resting, and taking care of me.

For a man like me, who quite frankly thrived on activity and engagement, sitting back during this critical time in my life felt like being at the top of a roller coaster I had never been on, but I knew that I didn't have many options. I was scared. I was uncertain. I had to raise my hands in the air and let go. The great challenge of this time for me was, in fact, letting go.

Once I did, what happened next was my own real-life miracle. I was buoyed. I was supported. I was lifted up, not only by an incredible family but also by my team, who literally ran a campaign to re-elect me while I was very much sitting in my living room and by my faith and a gracious, loving community. The hundreds of people who sent cards, notes, letters, cooked, visited with my family, did chores, and sent overwhelming good feelings of love to me, I'm convinced, in no small part, were instrumental in my healing. The time was a blur, but I attempted to read each and every message. One man sent a story about how dandelion root tea helped his wife reverse the effects of cancer. I added dandelion root tea to my daily regimen. I read and listened to people's heartfelt sentiments; I said my prayers and followed my health and medical routine. I let the election take care of itself, and I let life take its natural course. I didn't actively fight or engage with the disease. I simply surrendered, and I let myself get well.

Today, I am currently serving my third term as Mayor of Niagara Falls, Canada. I am healthy, well, and grateful beyond words. My family often says to me they can't believe how it all happened during that uncertain time in our lives. A fellow cancer survivor had told me early on that once this was over, I would never wish that it hadn't happened. These were very true words. I don't look at it as a curse, but rather, as a blessing.

To answer my own question, "what could I learn from this?" I have learned that resilience is sometimes letting go. This has made all the difference. It is true that the cork will always float to the top—as long as you don't hold it down.

*Jim Diodati*
**Mayor, City of Niagara Falls, Canada**

# Introduction

Resiliency is one of those words that hold a definition so powerful it literally moves lives from any tragedy to prosperity. Every person on this earth goes through various degrees of adversity, yet there is an underlying common trait applied that pulls people through and that is hope, or more specifically Belief, Faith, and Desire that life will get better.

It was through my own journey in life, I found enormous inspiration and hope by reading other people's success stories. Since I was a young girl, I had curiosity, my mom would call me the busy bumble-bee. As I grew into a young woman, I did not fit the status quo. You see, I had optimism and a great, loving home life. Yet, I faced bullying as a young girl, then became very resourceful as I learned of others who had suffered and healed through being resilient.

Whether you face health issues, medical issues, tragedy, loved ones hurting, loss; everyone's story matters. The journey is how you overcame struggles to become successful, from stories about people who came from war-torn countries to start a new life and achieve success beyond most would believe, to those who may have experienced pure hardship having experienced a major loss, like my very dear friend Roy Cleeves, who I watched go from almost bankrupt to owning his own real estate business, owning several real estate properties, and becoming a millionaire through his journey.

Stories have and always will inspire us! This idea of having a collection of many inspiring stories all in one book was a must for me. You see It is not about just one person. It is about how we all come together and inspire. I'm very blessed to have such amazing supportive people in my life including my realtor partner's Cindy and Roy, my husband and children, and my mom Gloria and my Dad in heaven who I miss dearly and what a man he was. My father was one of the most selfless men and inspired you to be the absolute best version of yourself possible. Have you tried and failed or just failed at trying? Plan your work and work your Plan were his two most favourite phrases. He taught us all how to fish vs giving the fish. He taught me the tools to survive and thrive in life.

So long as you have breath on this earth, you can inspire. Our stories give others hope and hope is how we heal, grow, and become stronger. Life will happen and it is how we react that makes the difference, what we learn, and how we grow from it. I live a very resilient life and feel I'm living some of my best chapters now and better are yet to come.

Keep inspiring, and allow others to know your story, you never know who you may impact,

*Michelle Carty*

# Chapter One

# *How I turned Hopelessness into Hopefulness*

⁓

### *Michael Ballard*

Life had suddenly and very unexpectedly come crashing down around me. However, I'm getting ahead of myself. There I was, married two years in, having just been promoted eight months prior and moving into my third career position on the east coast. These were exciting times; 7-figures of responsibility, 27 clients to consult with, and we'd purchased our first house! Wow, life was a whirlwind of things getting better and better and better. My bride and I had just settled into our neighbourhood, she'd landed a job, we'd found a house of worship to attend, life was good.

However, after two-plus weeks with a battle with what I thought was the flu, my life came crashing down. It was one of those: drag you down, beat you up, not going to let you up out of bed types of illness. Everything ached! I had never slept 20 hours a day before. And I knew I needed to get myself to the doctor's office immediately. There, they did blood tests, gave me a basic physical, and sent me to the hospital for another set of tests.

At the hospital, I was X-rayed and asked to stay around. A small team of medical professionals arrived within 30 minutes, and I was hustled into the ultrasound waiting room and bumped to the front of the line, ahead of all those pregnant ladies. There, they all crammed themselves into the room, and as the ultrasound was done once, twice, three times, I'd finally received a diagnosis. I was asked to drive directly to my gastroenterologist's office and was told he was waiting for me. Plus, oh yes, "we have an appointment for you at your family doctors tomorrow at 9:00 am, please be there; don't miss it."

Just over an hour later, my gastroenterologist informed me I had cancer in my lower digestive tract. Ouch. The next morning my family doctor told me she had been working the phones. "Michael, I have found out fortunately for you we have a very well trained Surgeon just across the bay in Halifax who has taken advanced training for what you're dealing with." I was to go the next day to meet Dr. George P. Konok, a surgeon and professor at Dalhousie University.

I'd just left the surgeon's office after being told I had cancer, in shock, yet all my life I was raised to assess, research, and reassess then create a plan of action, then take action. I got back to my car. There, I had a big cry of crocodile sized tears. Then, I knew it was time to take action. I drove to the family lawyers' office, where I got a new will drawn. My last one was two years old and done in another province. I recognized it was essential to have the proper paperwork up-to-date, to be safe, and to make things easier for my spouse.

Next was downstairs to see Peter, the real estate agent we'd bought our house from just a few months back. There, I shared all the family contact information, parents, brothers, work, and home. I drove home (the new will was in the mailbox already– with the bill) and put on the kettle to make a cup of tea. I sat there, as I let it steep, then poured the steaming water into my glass. I then went to my office and got out all of the vital paperwork. I put the life insurance, new will, real estate documentation, and other vital paperwork into an envelope and put an extra large clip on it, then I grabbed a large nail and hung it on the wall.

Now the tea is cool enough to drink. A plan. A plan. What do I need? What do we need? Support? I was already blessed to have a loving spouse, parents, siblings, and wonderful coworkers. What is next? Isolation in the hospital for several weeks. So, as I'd been taught, build a team. Ask for help. Ask for what you need.

I drove to my spouse's place of work to pick her up. had a big cry together, then I discussed the beginning of a plan I had started to formulate as I was in the lawyers' office. I was going to fight for his life. I wanted to prepare her as I started to plot and plan for the fight!

Once home, we both changed out of our workday clothes, and I freshen up with a shower and put on my comfy clothes. Then, off to my office. Time to put a team into place. I called those closest to me to ask for their help. I remember saying, "I don't want sympathy or empathy. Instead, I want you to share with me something upbeat and positive going on in your life, at home, or work.

Well, that causes a dam to burst. It was very very remarkable as the notes, cards, letters, and plants that all started to arrive at my home. One lady, a great friend of the family (Betty), sent me (in full bloom), a purple crocus in an upside-down gardening hat, with a pair of gardening gloves. Talk about sharing hope! My family are gardeners, my Dad had amazing gardens at my parent's home for well over 50 years. Purple for spirit, green for growth, gloves, and a hat for work to be done come spring. Out of the hundreds of things I got this one took the prize—so much symbolism.

Another big surprise was a very powerful and uplifting letter from the father of a co-worker. He wrote to me in a very elegant fashion and shared that both of his parents had had similar health issues, and lived well into their 80's. The insights shared, and the gift of hope in that letter has a very loving and beautiful place in my heart. What a gift to take the time to write a letter and send it out to a stranger. Thanks, Mel.

A key thing that helped me fight my cancer was building a team, asking for help, and specifying what I wanted during my battles and challenges ahead. Their gift of notes, cards, pictures, flowers, and so much more brought encouragement. To this day, it takes my breath away. Each person offered me hope, each helped me focus on the now, and each person helped me recognize that I'm resilient! Very powerful.

# Chapter Two

## Serene Cynthia Carty

∞

### Michelle Carty

I have always been a woman who liked to plan my work and work my plan. In 2003, I had a great career with triOS building their Ontario and Municipal government portfolio, a loving, supportive husband, two beautiful children, Joviann and Jeanelle, ages five and three. We had just moved into our 2nd home, and shortly after we decided we wanted to have one more child. I was in my late 30s and had it all planned out.

We were not loving the new house we recently moved into, so I put a plan together to purchase a 3rd home in pre-construction. We would move to our new home, and life would be wonderful, but the universe had a very different plan for me. May 2004, I got pregnant; we were thrilled. We had a year and a half before the new home would close, and everything was in place for our move.

On Nov 11, 2004, my life changed. I had a normal routine ultrasound test at McMaster Hospital and was admitted for observation. I felt great, it didn't make sense to me why I had to stay at the hospital. I had another test to do on Sunday and figured I was going home. After the test was completed, the nurse told me I was not going home, and I had to stay admitted for the remainder of my pregnancy term.

My husband went home to pick up clothes for me to stay. As I was in my room, I felt something strange, no pain, just strange. I called the nurse to check on me, and they immediately brought me to labour and delivery, hooked me up, and quickly advised my water was not broken yet fell through intact. They had me lay on the hospital bed, upside down so my feet and body were higher than my head, hoping my water would flow back, and they could hold off labour for a while. This made logical sense yet, I was in complete shock; all this was happening. My husband soon came back to the hospital with our girls. Every minute was paralyzing.

My parents arrived to pick up our kids, and by 8 pm that evening, I knew I was in labour. By 11 pm, the head of the NICU came in. They could not stop the labour, NICU told us due to my child being less than 26 weeks' gestation, we were having a micro-preemie. We were told she had a 50% chance of surviving and an 80% chance of having life-long issues, which could range from cerebral palsy, blindness, severe learning disorders, chronic lung disease, or paralyzation. Yet, the doctors could not intervene until we directed. It became our informed decision.

The next three hours were surreal, all that mattered was our belief and faith. My husband was incredible; he supported any decision I would have made, and he was by my side as we made this decision together. By 2:30 am, I told my husband they have to take her by c; the rest is up to our faith and eternal belief. They rushed me into surgery; I still remember every second of it. I could feel the pressure, all the medical team getting ready, and at 3:00 pm, we had a baby girl, I could hear her cry and got a glimpse of her, immediately the six doctors started working to keep her alive.

The next day we visited her in NICU, she was so tiny, weighing 490 grams, approximately 1 lb, so fragile. She was hooked up to a trach tube for breathing and had PICC lines in her. My heart and soul felt every second. The helplessness was unbearable. My husband and I were thrown so fast into this new world, and neither of us knew what the future would be. Yet we took it, minute by minute, hour by hour, and truly forced us to live in the now. Every cell in my body refused to believe she would not make it. The doctors even went as far as to inform us that because Serene was a girl and had black in her, she would stand a stronger chance of surviving based on statistics.

Nov 15, 2004, Serene Cynthia Carty was born. We named her after my husband's late mom Cynthia. Serene literally had to fight for her life. Her medical team told us she would have a 72-hour honeymoon phase; then, she would have one step forward and two steps back. I immediately had to do something, so the very day after I had Serene I pumped for two days straight, I was so determined (breast pump), and it paid off. By the end of the 2nd day, after hours of pumping, my milk came in.

When you have a child, it doesn't matter if they are term or preemie, that is your child. I just knew I loved every one of my children with unconditional love. I never once allowed the thought she was not coming home. I could only see the vision of her coming home. This journey of my life was brutal; it left me feeling helpless; it was gruelling. I structured the next three months by scheduling my 1-2 visits a day. I took care of my family and lived moment by moment. Serene had two blood transfusions, minor bleeding of the brain, and no immunities. She had a 4-hour surgery at 2 lbs and was on the trach breathing aspirator for five weeks with a CPAP device (inflating her lungs) for four weeks, the low flow for two days, and finally breathing on her own. She was tube fed from the beginning and learned how to breastfeed at 32 weeks (breath then suck then swallow), everything in life we learn.

The day we were finally able to bring Serene home, I had so much abundance of joy. We had to find a car bed because her little head was still too heavy for her body to hold up. Our beautiful Serene came home on Feb 17, 2005, at 4 lbs and 3 oz. We took turns sleeping for the first few weeks to make sure she was breathing. Three weeks after we brought her home, we successfully sold our house, and by July 2005, and moved into our 3rd new home. Serene was the longest baby and toddler we ever had; she is our miracle child. Our beautiful daughter is now 15-years-old and she is doing amazing!

Serene is an angel; she has taught us so much, especially her calm patience and love for everyone. Her emotional intelligence is incredible. We can all take a few lessons from our children. They are here to teach us. This journey and how we held each other up during these times taught me just how strong we are as a family. Serene has impacted so many people over her 15 years, and we are so incredibly blessed to be her parents. I see amazing things for Serene in her future, and she gives me strength every day.

# Chapter Three

## *Travelling Through Adversity*

*Cheryl Zhang*

The adversity that you go through in your life makes you strong enough to face your dreams! The struggle is real; like anyone else, I have faced my share of obstacles. I believe that adversity is what creates such a powerful force for us to learn. My challenges have allowed me to work harder towards all of my goals. I have gained determination and inner strength within my mind to keep pushing forward!

I lost my grandparents when I was only one-year-old. Some of the key indicators of my willpower have come from loss and pain. I have gone through emotional abuse, physical abuse, and financial setbacks from being involved with men who did not have my best interest at heart. I've been so hurt that some days, it was hard to get out of bed to face the world. I was bullied by my exes and told that I was not smart enough to be an author. In grade 5, I was picked on and made fun of plenty of times, too many to count.

At the age of six-years-old, I managed to get a spring caught in my mouth between my teeth and my gums. I still remember crying so loud in pain, my grandfather came running to me, and he had to pull it out with pliers. He was such a caring man to help me that day.

I got hit by a car when I was only seven-years-old while I was riding my bike down the middle of the road. My parents always told me to stay on the sidewalk, but this one day, I was daring, and I disobeyed them. I was so all shook up, but I recovered.

When I was in Grade 6, I sat in bubblegum, and it was all over my pants. I was wearing white jeans, and it made such a mess. I still remember the kids laughing at me.

I was told by my parents to come home before dark, and I rebelled against that one night. Around 9 pm, a truck pulled up, and a man got out of it. He was trying to pull me into his truck, I kicked him in the leg, and I managed to get away from him. When I got home, I told my parents about it, and I was grounded for one week. I was only 12-years-old and so glad that I was ok. Whew!

For many years, I had a speech impairment, and it lasted until about Grade 7. I would always speak differently in class, and the kids would tease me about it. Even my teachers would poke at me, and I was forced into attending a special class once a week for speech therapy. They would mock and laugh at me when it was time for me to go to my speech for the day!

Once, I got into a car accident with my baby sister when we were on our way to the beach from my parent's house. The car started to slide on the soft shoulder; it tipped over sideways into the ditch. The water was pouring in, I was crying, breathing heavily and my sister was crying too. The water was coming in and suctioned the door to stay closed. I managed to get it open so we could get out.

Financial struggles are something I have struggled with for many years, starting right after high school with credit card debt and a lack of savings. I lived with a mindset of lack. Controlling boyfriends told me that I wasn't good enough to achieve all of my amazing goals and dreams that I had for my life! Those seeds always stuck with me.

I got a major tooth infection and had an allergic reaction to the antibiotics that I was prescribed. I woke up with sharp pains, and my head was swollen. I was up all night in massive pain. I needed emergency dental surgery that same day! For many years I have had acne-prone skin, breakouts, freckles, and I was teased about having pimples on my face. I was hit by a bridge bus when I was walking to the mall and crossed the street, and the bus ran the red light and hit me. I was bruised up pretty badly on both of my legs.

I had recently had a miscarriage in November of 2019 when I was almost done my first trimester of pregnancy. I was obviously devastated by it. The road to resilience was not easy. I finally got enlightened with strength when I went to college to become an Insurance Advisor. I gained the courage to publish my first book called *Treasures Within Our Heart.*

I'm now a motivational author of 11 motivational books, and I have published them all in the last few years. I am discovering that I can be weak, strong, scared, and brave all at the same time. It is never too late to follow your amazing dreams to create the life that you crave for yourself, and I am living proof that you can achieve anything!

Keep smiling, keep dreaming, keep believing in yourself, and you will see miracles happen in your life. You'll see your dreams come true for you! You do really hold the magical key to open the doors to all of your dreams. It started with me living with a mindset and attitude of gratitude for this beautiful life. It all starts with you!

# Chapter Four

## *Ashes*

∞

### *Jonathan Tarrant*

*"The Longer You Hold Your Secrets,*
*The More They Gain Disproportionate Power Over You"*

I couldn't see all the raging beauty and love that surrounded me. I felt small and frail, but I almost never showed it. Much of my life has been spent in a state of feeling insecure and ungrounded. I suppose that feeling comes from my childhood and the way I grew up.

I'm an only child, and my folks moved us around quite regularly. Grade 3 was my first experience with this, and it was awful. We moved halfway through the school year, away from all the friends and familiar places I'd grown up with and into a crappy little town with a much rougher crowd than I was accustomed to. It was shocking, at the time. I began acting out, talking back, and getting into trouble. I didn't understand any of it. I felt very alone.

My parents behaved in ways I could not understand as a child. One of the biggest issues was their lack of money. They wanted to protect me from stress and anxiety and allow me to have my childhood. I respect their good intentions, but I could see my parents were hiding something from me. This was all very unsettling, and I quickly began to detach myself from them.

Over time and through more moves, I learned to close myself off. Somehow, I got the idea that I was weird, and a bad person. I carried these ideas around, and I didn't know how to talk about it with anyone, least of all my parents. I became painfully self-conscious, and isolated within myself. I'd also become good at hiding it.

As a young man, I presented an image that was much cooler and stronger than how I felt on the inside. Only when the pressure was on, my armor often failed me. I constantly felt trapped, frustrated, overwhelmed, and powerless. I thought it was my life that I was unhappy with but really it was me. I'd become disconnected from my soul and from my better judgement.

Later, I had many great things in my life and a marriage which was nicer than what I'd ever imagined. Yet, part of me was always dissatisfied. There was a tremendous conflict between what I desired from life and what my small self-image was telling me.

There was no-one to talk to, because I had secretly shut everyone out. I was afraid to admit my deepest thoughts and fears, so they remained within me, festering. In my heart, I knew I was out of control and I was ashamed of who I'd become. I didn't know how to get out of it. I didn't know how to be really vulnerable or open.

I spent decades being uncomfortable in my own skin, with lots of internal beliefs that had me on a self-destructive path, without me fully realizing it. I acted out my poor self-image more and more. I often behaved in ways that went against the strong advice of my intuition. I'd become accustomed to ignoring that advice, regardless of how loud it was, and this contributed to me feeling gross, disconnected and unhappy with myself.

I was unable to see myself clearly, or be fully honest with myself. I was in denial about the harm my choices were doing to my family and to myself, but they were still my choices.

I wanted out of that life, but couldn't bear the thought of taking responsibility. I couldn't stand the idea of letting my family down like that, of failing, of losing all my comforts and fending for myself. I didn't feel strong enough. Then literally overnight everything changed. I had to leave the house and in the morning, there I was, in the cold of March in Toronto looking for a place to live and straining to get my head around all the consequences and challenges that were barreling towards me. Everything I'd been holding in for so long, suddenly came gushing out all at once. It was as if I'd never experienced emotions before at full strength. Now I was drowning in their intensity. I can only imagine what it must have been like for my family and friends.

Resilience found me while I was completely broken and felt like suicide would be a welcome relief from all the pain, shame and anxiety. It was the shock of it all and the dismay that finally opened my eyes. I could clearly see exactly how I'd brought myself to that place. Amongst all the overwhelming chaos and heartbreak, though, part of me actually felt relief.

I sought out some good, solid help and discarded my pride. As I collected and reassembled myself, I began to reconnect with my soul and my intuition. I left out the parts that didn't serve me and I questioned everything I'd ever believed about myself. So much of what I thought I knew about me had been wrong! I learned to lean into the uncertainty of life. Whereas before, I was averse to change and always afraid of the worst. Uncertainty is where the magic is!

I've attracted mentors, coaches, and many inspiring, uplifting new friends. I've listened deeply to my inner voice of truth and continue to do so. I've allowed the real me to shine and show himself. I've found bravery, resilience, and integrity. I've developed a sense of gratitude for every experience I've ever had, and I know that I needed a massive, supernova blast to get me here.

**In my darkest time, I found my resilience.**

What is light without darkness? Both are necessary. Each gives context and power to the other. The brightness I've discovered within myself, inspires me to share my experience with the world. My breakdown gave me the gift of clarity to create my brand, **Live-More.**

The path of Live-More leads you to a significantly more powerful, wholehearted relationship with yourself, and the world. From Live-More, I've produced an online course named the Lost and Found Man. The course is aimed at men because it can be very challenging to break out of the stereotypes and social expectations we face. A man who is comfortable with himself, connected to his heart and able to express himself, will serve his family and friends at a high level.

My mission is to make tremendous positive cultural change in the world, starting with men and serving all people. Now I know I'm resilient, and I'm committed to sharing what I've learned.

Let's connect!

# Chapter Five

## *Grow Through What You Go Through*

❦

### *Thea Cosma*

When I was growing up, moving was a consistent experience. I moved from one neighbourhood to another, then one city to next, and eventually from one country to another. It was very stressful, especially as a child because I had to constantly adapt and make new friends. It seemed that my life had a plan to uproot my environment frequently. The only voluntary move I made was in my twenties when I took a leap of faith emigrating from Europe to Canada. By that time, change and adjustment had become a theme in my life.

As a child, I felt anxious, upset, fearful, confused, and not able to digest my emotions properly. In my way, I learned to adapt but became shy and naturally wanted to be liked and make new friends. During high school, I attended four different schools. I completed high school in another country, having to learn a new language, make new friends, and adjust to a foreign culture. As a teenager, challenges seemed like mountains, new experiences seemed like a punishment, and resentment seemed like a normal emotion.

As war erupted in my homeland, my family emigrated from Cyprus to the UK, where we found more peace and a new normal. However, I was longing for comfort and stability, so food and especially chocolate became my best friends. There is something about English chocolate that one cannot resist. So, a chubby teenager trying to figure it out, not knowing where I belonged, sandwiched between two cultures. Fear was a constant companion at that time, but as I started to grow, evolve, and adapt, everything seemed to flow smoother.

Change, fear, and uncertainty taught me to bounce back, become resilient, break away from the familiar and trust in the unknown. Through struggles, I became stronger just like the song "what doesn't kill you makes you stronger." Sometimes, wisdom comes through change and pain.

Just when I thought I settled in with my new life in the UK, another circumstance pushed me to move yet again to a new continent. In my twenties, I met my future husband, who was a Canadian, which led me to make Toronto my permanent home. I became equipped with all the skills of moving and adjusting. The transition was a lot easier than in my younger years, but I still had to recreate every aspect of my life. Through strength and trusting myself, I learned to build new foundations as required and navigate my feelings and emotions.

By the time I was in Canada, I already conquered most of my fears of anything foreign and unfamiliar. My new journey has begun. Settling into our first home, designing and decorating became a pleasant activity. As time passed, everything fell into place, a job, children which lead to a fast-paced, robotic western lifestyle. The responsibilities of a job, family, and overall life started to weigh me down. My health was deteriorating, and there was no joy through the journey of life. It was time to reflect and declutter what was no longer serving me. I was forced to take time out, and the job was first to disappear. I needed to reset my lifestyle, allow peace and balance to be present again.

With my corporate job behind me, new possibilities and opportunities started to emerge. Letting go of what no longer served me, allowed my creativity and spirituality to surface. Interior Design, Feng Shui, Reiki, Qi Gong, and other modalities were part of my studies. My life purpose was becoming a reality; I was stepping into a more authentic version of myself. Breaking the cycle of the norm takes courage, persistence, and trust that all is well.

An unexpected disruption into my family's routine was moving from Toronto to Calgary, Alberta. It felt like another foreign country with its laws, regulations, and culture. This time it was my two teenage boys that had to deal with uprooting their world. We reluctantly moved to Alberta due to my husband's job, not expecting any benefit in it. The beginning is always tricky, but eventually, we all settled into our own schedules.

Nature in Alberta was mesmerizing; visiting the picturesque Lake Louise and the golden Rocky mountains for the first time was breathtaking. Wild animals were part of everyday life; coyotes, deers, large rabbits lived in the parks and all over the city. Living close to nature brings back balance and harmony into our being. Appreciating the trees, the grass, the wind, even the insects and witnessing how each living thing is contributing to Earth is life-altering.

Little did I know that I would grow and evolve so much in the West. I found myself drawn to various metaphysical and spiritual teachings. My intuition heightened, I furthered my knowledge on Feng Shui, Dowsing, connected with like-minded individuals and groups. As I look back, I realize the move turned out to be instrumental for the whole family. My boys were exposed to another environment, which made them more resilient, adaptable, and grateful. Change is not an enemy; it is a catalyst for growth - so embrace the change.

Life in the West lasted five years; Toronto was calling us back, so we made a conscious decision to return with no regrets. Upon arriving, it was time to re-evaluate our friendships and become more aware of our choices to enable peace and tranquility to be part of us. "Letting go" became my mantra; no need to hold on to anyone or anything that keeps us in the past or brings us down was a fundamental lesson for me.

With every move, there is upheaval. With every move, there is also growth and transformation. Believing and trusting that everything happens for a reason, our whole perspective on life can shift in an uplifting way. As we continue to explore, experience, evolve, we learn, grow, gain wisdom, and valuable skills through the University of Life.

# Chapter Six

## *Kreature*

❦

### *Ryan Gumbert*

At a young age, I was given the opportunity of a lifetime. However, without the proper knowledge, the opportunity could never be a success. It was a great lesson to learn at such a young age as it helped shape me as I grew into an adult.

My brother and I made the decision that we would own a gas station, convenience store, propane refill centre, and a fitness gym in a small town. It would be just the two of us running all these businesses together, with literally zero knowledge at the time about how to effectively do so at the time. As you can probably predict, this didn't turn out the way we had hoped.

We ran the business for just over a year or so until we were overwhelmed and well in over our heads. I had never been so stressed in my life as I juggled all these ventures and worked hours on hours on end, with little to no sleep. Ultimately we ended up selling the business and moved back to our home town Hamilton, Ontario, where I stayed with a long time friend, renting out his basement apartment. I wasn't sure what to do at this point because I didn't have my high school diploma; I was short, just one credit.

I knew I wanted to go to college one day, but I wasn't sure what course I wanted to take, and on top of that, I was unsure if I could even get into college without having my high school diploma. My friends and family supported me as I decided to inquire with a few people and found out I could indeed apply, I just had to write an equivalency test. My next decision was to figure out what I wanted to take. I was very anxious about making that decision as it was going to determine my future and I had so much uncertainty in regards to what I wanted to do with my life. Eventually, I decided to go to college for Marketing but was very nervous about my decision.

Going to college for marketing was the start of everything that was to come and one of the best decisions I ever made. At school, I learned all the necessary business skills needed to run a successful company of my own the next time around. Or so I thought. I ended up starting a small business creating 3D virtual tours with two of my close friends, applying the mastermind principle. We invested loads of time into the business, and we even got a government grant with our business idea. We secured some really great clients, and at the time, I thought I'd be doing that line of work for the rest of my life. Unfortunately, we had a fallout in our friendship, and the business crumbled in a blink of an eye. Once again, I had a major opportunity fall apart, and I was left with nothing to show for all the work.

The result of the fallout drifted me towards being stuck in a nine to five sales job afterward, where I was really unhappy. Although I was making good money, I had no true passion for the job at hand until I was once again presented with a great opportunity, this time through a coworker, who presented me with the idea to work for an amazing company, CC Realty Group. I started as an inside sales agent and had intentions of becoming a real estate agent, but eventually transitioned into a marketing role within the company. This was a whole new beginning.

Through CC Realty Group, I had the opportunity to reignite a long lost passion of mine, graphic, and web design. I've always had a knack for creating and designing things on a computer. I actually made my first website for a business when I was 13-years-old, and I started using photoshop and editing videos when I was 11-years-old. I enjoyed doing these things but considered them more like hobbies.

As I excelled in assisting CC Realty Group South's growth, I started opening my mind to turning this hobby into an actual career. I took everything I learned over all those years of failing and applied it with a hobby that I have a passion for, website design and digital marketing. That's when the company I now own was made: **Kreature.**

**Kreature** allowed me to express my creativity through a hobby that I love and getting to call it my career was the cherry on top. Still, with all the knowledge I had obtained through my experiences, I had uncertainties. Owning **Kreature** would mean that business owners are trusting and relying on me for themselves to make a living. I was nervous I couldn't deliver the results and that I wasn't as good as I thought I was. Still, I pushed through and eventually started working with a great client base. I started realizing my self worth as I was helping other business owners surpass goals and expectations!

The most amazing part about where I'm at now is I have the proper knowledge to be successful and help others achieve outstanding results using the knowledge I've obtained through all of my losses. My story of resiliency is a story of turning my losses into lessons. The best part about it all is when it comes to my everyday work; designing websites, editing videos, creating social ad campaigns, it's something I'm truly passionate about, and it doesn't feel like work when I'm doing it!

When I look back at all the failures I went through and the stresses I endured through life's uncertainties, I can see now that If I didn't encounter all those moments in my journey, I would have never been able to make it to where I am today, and for that, I am thankful for my resiliency.

# Chapter Seven

## *Rebuilding My Name*

⌒⌒

### *Cleoni Crawford*

I had been acting quite odd for about a month before I fell into my first depression. I didn't want to eat, comb my hair, get out of bed, or even brush my teeth. I simply wanted to escape my life. It was a horrible feeling, one that I had never experienced before. However, once I checked myself into the Centre for Addiction and Mental Health, and heard my diagnosis, I was on my journey towards health.

It was 2006, and I was in my final year at the University of Toronto when I first learned the term bipolar, never imagining that it would be something that I would have to wear. I spent six months in therapy for bipolar and finally started to get better. However, one day, I decided to tell a church sister that I was happy that I finally knew what was happening with my health, she responded, "No sister, don't receive it, that is of the devil." So, for the next six years when I would have episodes, I would brush it off as an attack from the devil.

Things took a turn for the worst in 2012. I had lost my government job, my fashion business was plummeting, and I lost my apartment due to a flood. With all that was going on at one time, my mother became very concerned and ordered me to check myself in the hospital. At first, I fought the idea but eventually, I went. This would not be the first time that I would be hospitalized. In fact, it would be 26 times in total. During this time, my life was unstable, and I found myself in and out of shelters, imprisoned, and suicidal.

The chaos continued until one day when I decided to look myself in the mirror and say, "My name is Cleoni Crawford and I have bipolar and that is okay." Once I said those words, things started to improve. I started to take medication and my life improved tremendously.

The following year, I decided that I would take a program at George Brown College called Transition to Post-Secondary Education. This program was designed to help you go back to school or work. The courses were so good and helped me to become introspective. I found myself getting better and better. I also took a 16-week course called Laughing Like Crazy where I would learn how to turn my painful life experiences into jokes. By the end of this course, I was found to be hilarious. I realized I was loved and I was starting to love myself again.

After real change began to unfold, I decided that I would create a talk show to raise awareness for mental health. Considering that there was not a show like this at the time, people were quite supportive of it. I was able to raise money and awareness for the show and completed a total of 20 YouTube interviews. I even recorded the first pilot episode for the show. My life was turning around and I was proud of myself.

I submitted the episode onto YesTV to be aired in February 2015 and unfortunately was told that the audio was too low and that I would need to resubmit. So, I scheduled a date to resubmit and exactly one day before the re-taping I was hospitalized again by my mother. I was bitter. How could she do this to me? I must be cursed. Finally, after two weeks I was released but now became suicidal again. During this time, I decided that I would check myself into CAMH again and get the help I needed. It took three weeks but I finally started to heal and was released again. I was supposed to come back to CAMH for a 28-

day treatment program but rather than do that, I decided that I would leave the province and run from it all.

From here, I went to Ottawa, Montreal, New Brunswick, and then finally my destination point of Nova Scotia. When I arrived, I was so happy. I felt like this was home. I stayed in a women's shelter since I had no money and then after a week was sadly asked to leave. Eventually, I was hospitalized again but this time I was treated badly by the security officers and the nurses, which made me decide that I wanted to leave.

So, one day, while given a pass to leave the hospital for a few hours, I decided that I was not going to come back till a few days since it was Easter and I wanted the weekend to myself. I packed a few of my things and dressed in layers so I would have a change of clothing and left the hospital. Since my disability cheque came in, I decided that I would stay in a hotel and pamper myself. Once I came out of the shower, I started to relax and then I heard the word, "run." So, I packed up my clothing and went to the VIA Rail station as I was going to escape from the mental hospital. I boarded the train and kept my phone on airplane mode until I got to New Brunswick.

When I arrived in New Brunswick, I decided that I would give the hospital a courtesy call and let them know that I had escaped from the hospital. The police were contacted and within hours, my face was plastered all over CBC news. Considering all the work I had done in mental health, this was devastating to me. This was the first negative article that had been written about me in the media. Sadly, I was captured in Montreal, sent to a mental hospital, and hospitalized for two weeks. After those two weeks, I was given the option to stay in Montreal or go back to Ontario to be hospitalized for 30 more days. Frustrated and tired, I decided that I would go back home.

It took some time to get back to a place where things would be stable, but I can now say that I have bounced back. Despite my challenges, I am now a mental health advocate where I share my story, have written a book detailing my journey called *The Music of My Life*, have started a podcast to help others share their journey, and in school studying mental health and addictions so I can help others. If you want to talk about resilience, you can now call me Queen.

# Chapter Eight

## *Keep Calm And Carry On*

⤬

### *Connie Whitmore*

I have had a long career as a management consultant, and like any career, it has had its ups and downs. I have worked in large companies, small companies, and as an independent consultant. I have had the privilege of working on contracts in North America, Japan, Europe, and the Caribbean. All very different challenges and some amazing experiences.

Throughout that career, I have learned that the most important thing that provides strength and resilience is the thoughts that you harbour in your own head. These you can control. Find your source of strength and resilience within you. Psychologists tell us that depression is a feeling that you are not in control. Take that control.

**Have self-confidence:**

Look at yourself objectively and know your strengths and weaknesses. Don't ever forget your strengths and learn to overcome your weaknesses. From an early age, I knew that I had a brain that worked pretty well in academic environments, and in analyzing and problem-solving. I had confidence there. I was, however, socially quite shy coming out of high school, less so coming out of university. People who know me now find that quite hard to believe. I leveraged the confidence I had in my thinking abilities, to overcome my weakness in social circumstances. I spoke to clients and potential clients, I spoke up at meetings, and I spoke publicly at conferences. I had something to say, and people listened. It is a matter of confidence and practice. I have not been constrained by shyness for a long time now.

Knowledge can be acquired academically or on the job. But you gain competence through experience. Do not sell yourself short just because you may not have the academic credentials that others do or because you do not have certain professional accreditations. No matter what way you have acquired your knowledge, what matters is how well you apply it. I have known individuals with MBAs who could never manage a company and individuals with a PMP (Project Management Professional) designation who would fail at managing projects. One of the most gifted project managers I know does not have a university degree but has years of experience managing large-scale successful projects. The ability to effectively apply your knowledge means a lot more than how you acquired it.

View yourself as succeeding. Sports psychologists know that the outcome you envision is the outcome you get. They help athletes view themselves as succeeding when they are competing. I played golf with someone who panicked whenever he saw a water hazard. He was convinced his ball would go in the water. When he hit the ball, where do you think it went? In life and at work, you need to visualize that the ball hits the destination you are targeting. Have confidence in your knowledge and abilities and know that they can be applied to a myriad of new opportunities.

**Do not blame others or circumstances.**

If you find yourself in a difficult situation, do not blame others or circumstances for the difficulty. It is what it is. Blame is just a waste of energy. Spend that energy on finding a positive outcome for your situation. Again, step outside yourself and look at the situation objectively. What courses of action are possible? Which one do you choose? If you find yourself in an impossible situation with no visible positive outcome, you still have one good option—you can leave the situation entirely—your choice. And you can move on to something else that is positive.

When working for a large company, I was managing a business unit within a local office. My business unit was profitable. My unit financials would be forwarded to the head office through the local office. One year, new executives came in to manage the local office— their financials were not looking good—they had too much overhead, too many managers who were not bringing in revenue. So before the financials went to the head office, they transferred some of their overhead to my business unit. They looked better and all of a sudden, I had a significant loss that was not mine. A colleague of mine told me he had heard them conspiring to do this, and I confirmed that it was true. I could accuse the local executives of fiddling the books, but I did not think that would go well. Instead, I negotiated my way out of the company. Those local executives knew that I knew what they had done, but nothing was said between us. It helped me negotiate good terms for departure. I went on to something more positive and an environment that was ethical.

When I have recounted this story, some have expressed the opinion that this happened to me because I am a woman. I do not agree with that view. It happened to me because those executives were unscrupulous and because they could. I ran the only business unit reporting to them, and they controlled the final financials that went to head office.

I never saw the workplace divided into "women and men." I focused on role and competence, the latter being quite important to earn my respect. I never felt disadvantaged in the workplace because of my gender. I did not look for it and only rarely found it. I think that if you are looking for something, then you find it—sometimes even if it is not there. Certainly, there were men I encountered who probably thought I was somehow not 'as good,' but I really did not care what they thought. It only mattered what they did, and even that did not matter as long as their actions did not impact my career and what I wanted to do. I have worked in male-dominated industries (defense) and in male-dominated societies (Japan) and have been successful. Make sure you carry confidence and assume that there is no bias until you find out otherwise. If you find it, deal with it. If it is systemic to the organization, leave.

I hope that my advice and experiences give my readers food for thought and help them navigate their careers. Good luck out there!

# Chapter Nine

## *Turn Your Pain Into Power*

∽⊗∾

### *Jessica De Serre Boissonneault*

October 12th, 2012, is the day that transformed my life. Any parent can attest to that. For me, it was the day the beast in me was awoken— that lioness, a loving individual who will do whatever it takes to protect my daughter. The moment I became a mom, I held my daughter and knew I was transformed. I had to be strong now. That's when I decided to turn pain into power.

In summer 2013, Josiana was eight-months-old, and my maternity leave was coming to an end. At the time, I was staying in North Carolina with my husband, our daughter, and my mother-in-law. Things were toxic in the house, and it was extremely difficult for me to endure. I was tired, nervous, and stressed.

I was supposed to go back to my work in August that year, which meant I had to leave my daughter in North Carolina and fly to Toronto. I didn't want to be away from my daughter. I wasn't comfortable leaving her because I did not trust her dad. I asked myself, "What is the solution?" The answer: I am strong. God is there. This was the key moment of turning my pain into power.

I made the bold decision to go back to University and moved into a small one-bedroom apartment, taking all the stuff I needed from North Carolina. My mom got me furniture and helped as much as she could. My sister and friends were also there to support me. During the process of moving, I focused on those blessings instead of focusing on the struggles.

How did I survive financially? I asked for loans and bursaries from the government because I had no help in the money department, and I was already supporting my husband, our daughter, and my mother-in-law. That decision for me was the best. I could not leave my baby girl, and I could not be so far away from her. So, I trusted my family and friends to be there for me. I also was able to find a babysitter that would watch my daughter any time of the day, which was a major blessing and solution during the times I was on call at work, in classes, or at school sometimes evening. I also had to take a job on the weekend to make ends meet. This was my reality, university, taking the bus, getting home; cooking, bathing the baby, and putting her to bed. After I finished cleaning the kitchen and the floors, I would sit at the table with my laptop and study. I remember like it was yesterday. Yet, this was seven years ago. How was I able to get up every morning? I used the pain of struggle. That pain and struggle, I turned into strengths. I used the vision; I had to complete my degree: determination and perseverance.

December came and I was at the end of the semester with all my final exams. I had to get ready to go back to work after being off for 15 months. I was terrified. The day I was driving to the training center, I was shaking in my car. I wanted to turn around and say I couldn't do it. It felt like I didn't have enough time to study for my exams and I was anxious that I wouldn't remember practical drills.

When I arrived at the center, I sat down, and immediately wanted to leave. Breathe Jessica; you are here. They assigned me to a position where I had to take the lead, and it was one of the most terrifying moments of my life. I had not been working for so long. I was exhausted. I was stressed out. I was dealing with so much in my personal life. The only thought I had was that I couldn't do it. What ended up happening that day? An angel called Chantal (a colleague of mine) took me aside, looked into my eyes, and so authentically, she reminded me I could do this. She gave me a hug, and at that moment, I chose to let go of the stress.

By the time Christmas came that year, I was dealing with the December final exams. I was busy at my job on the weekends because of the holidays, and I was struggling financially. I could barely afford much food, so forget about Christmas gifts. Thank god for credit cards.

Fast forward to April 2014, I wrote my final exam to complete my bachelor's degree. I remember like it was yesterday. I came down multiple staircases, sat in my car parked outside, and cried my eyes out! My body was shaking. I could not believe I had made it. I could not believe I persisted. I could not believe I had completed my degree until the last exam. I was resilient!

When I talk about turning pain into power, I'm specifically talking about the fact that I struggled in so many areas of my life. I struggled financially. I struggled to be a new mom, and a single mom. I struggled with a toxic marriage and eventually a divorce. I struggled with moving into a new apartment with no car or furniture. I struggled with a very unstable work schedule being on call. I struggled with being alone. I struggled with having a second job. I struggled to take the bus to bring my daughter to the babysitter. I struggled to have my daughter full time with not much support. I struggled to be full-time at the University. And I struggled to build myself again. However, I had a vision. I had a vision of living a life filled with happiness. I had a vision of working towards being the best version of myself. I had a vision of completing the things I started. I was going to finish my university degree, no matter what.

My message to all of you readers is to keep persisting. Resiliency comes when you persist. Focus on your vision, and your end goal. Focus on what is important, and your blessings. We will all go through pain, remember always turn your pain into power.

# Chapter Ten

## Anxiety, Addiction & Accountability

∽

### Katie McDermott

*"Life is too short to spend another day at war with yourself"*
—Rita Ghatourey

I was born the oldest of three in Omaha, NE on Dec 15th, 1983, breach, shriveled skin, and with dislocated hips. To fix my hips, I was wrapped up in three diapers and sent home. In addition to the hip deformity, anxiety was there to accompany me since day one. Growing up, I found it hard to socialize, always feeling as though there was a knot of unbearable fear inside me. I lacked the confidence to talk to people, worried about possibly being teased or not accepted.

Anxiety wasn't all bad though, it benefited me in accomplishing things like not being late, and keeping things orderly, to the extent of obsessive-compulsive thought patterns. I also struggled with the inability to express my own thoughts and beliefs, afraid to speak up or ask for guidance. I felt like an outsider, wandering through life, lost, and afraid.

Entering my teenage years, it was even more challenging to find where I belonged, as everyone I knew from my childhood years seemed to have suddenly put on a façade to gain approval and acceptance. I silently wandered the halls past girls who used to be friends, yet would no longer talk or even acknowledge me. I tried and it was too exhausting to behave in an unauthentic manner, so I kept to myself.

Soon after I discovered my solution to all my problems--alcohol and drugs. I discovered what I had been missing my whole life. The sickly-sweet smooth liquid poured down my throat and provided a sense of solace. I started to party very hard, would sneak out at night, and wake up and do it again. I put my parents through some major stress and worry. But at the time it didn't matter, all I cared about was chasing this feeling, this high, this pure level of ecstasy.

Having found the solution to suppress the uneasiness inside me, I rapidly began drinking every weekend, then progressed to weeknights, all through high school. I also dabbled in various drugs, and whatever else just happened to land in my path, I said yes to because It was my answer to everything.

The substance abuse continued throughout my young adult years, I moved into a party house with six other people. It was a party 24/7. During this time, I had some significant experiences; I found myself at the barrel end of a gun two different times, both were robberies; I was sexually molested in a handful of incidents, sometimes right in the open at parties and other times in private; I stole from others and lied about it, and abused my own body in countless ways. I never allowed myself to process anything, I used the closest form of mind-altering substance and moved on.

Eventually, I moved into an apartment in a rundown area and pursued a culinary degree. At 21, I became pregnant with my son, Silvan. I was sober throughout my pregnancy but quickly resumed drinking after he was born. A couple of years later, living in a nicer part of town, I gave birth to my daughter Eliani. Again, I was sober throughout my pregnancy, and quickly back at the bottle as soon as I could. The drugs had mostly stopped at this point unless they were prescribed. After her birth, I went back to college and got a business degree and I was hired at a very large and renowned company. By this point, I was drinking nearly every day. I needed no reason to drink, basically living was a reason for me to drink.

A year into my corporate career, I started having major hip pains. I saw a doctor who said it was my back, not my hips, and sent me away with pain pills. I visited her every month and the same thing happened repeatedly for two years. At this time, I discovered the magic of mixing pain meds and alcohol, and I actually made a conscious choice to keep doing them, with the attitude that I would stop when I wanted to. The hip pain worsened to the point where I got a second opinion. That doctor diagnosed me with hip dysplasia and sent me to another doctor to perform a procedure called a Periacetabular osteotomy. Basically, restructured my hip socket, put my femur in the right place, and fastened me back together with 4 titanium screws. After the surgery, I had so many pain meds. my addiction continued and worsened. During the weeks, I would suffer at work through cold sweats, at times curling up in the corner of the bathroom to try and power nap to feel better.

The outside of my life appeared to be perfectly normal. I had two kids, a good job, a home, a dog. I took care of my children providing for them, spending time with them, reading bedtime stories, attending family gatherings, all the while under the influence. Internally, I was slowly deteriorating, becoming physically, emotionally, and mentally beat down. All the bottled feelings and guilt were literally tearing me apart inside. I had become severely depressed, constantly anxious, and I hated who I was.

In September 2012, I sat on my bedroom floor, defeated and uncontrollably sobbing, I knew I could no longer survive this lifestyle. I was either going to stop or die. By the grace of a higher power, I was given the strength to ask for help. I decided to go to an inpatient treatment facility, checked in on September 18th, extremely intoxicated and high on pills, puking due to the amount of substances in my system. September 19th, 2012 I was sober, in a detox facility, four days later I moved into treatment. I spent 30 days learning how to live a sober life, finding out who I was and what was needed to do to maintain my sobriety along with living life on life's terms. The most important lesson I learned is that I am not in control, I have to surrender and accept whatever comes my way.

After leaving the treatment facility I found a local support group and started regularly attending. I met others in that group, who I found were completely different than me but we all suffered from the same disease: addiction. In these groups, I slowly started to learn how to live a sober life. I had to learn how to do everything sober. My anxiety spiked and my self-esteem was completely obliterated.

Over the next few years, I started to transform the shell of a human I had become. I intensely reviewed the wreckage of my past, facing my deeply buried inner demons. I had to process all the emotions I never allowed myself to feel before. I learned healing, forgiveness, grace, humility, unconditional love, and acceptance. I made amends to those who were in my destructive pathway, including self-forgiveness. I learned to love who I was, in every single facet, which is not easy but is imperative. These lessons and actions gradually turned into a miraculous relief of the compulsion to drink and drug.

Today I am re-born, blessed in knowing who I am at the innermost depths of my soul. I have the ability to accept life as it transpires. I choose not to wallow in the misery of the past. When life presents challenges, I process my emotions without becoming attached to them. I also practice gratitude for every moment in my life, honoring myself and the beautiful moments I experience while alive on this earth. I have the choice to let that brick take me down or I can take it and build myself up.

Life in recovery is simply a daily reprieve, there is no cure but I am granted one day at a time based on holding myself accountable for my own actions, thoughts, and words. I have the power to grow by putting one foot in front of the other moving on even in the darkest of moments, one day, one hour, one minute, one second at a time.

# Chapter Eleven

## *Beautifully Blended & Empowered*

❦

### *Tina Clements*

*"Strength and growth come only through
continuous effort and struggle."*
*—Napoleon Hill*

I want parents out there to know that there are alternatives. I didn't learn this until a few years ago when I was thrust into a life-changing event where I felt I wasn't prepared but knew I had to step up.

It was a chance meeting that beautiful sunny day in July. I didn't feel like attending an old friend's surprise birthday party, but my friend kept insisting I go with her. As I mingled and chatted, I was introduced to my friend's oldest brother. He was good looking, very nice, and recently separated. He had two adorable kids, a little girl the same age as my son and a younger son, by just 18 months.

After the party, I called him and asked him out. He accepted and that night - It was like a lightning bolt hit us - Love. Neither one of us had ever felt this way. I'd only been married for a short time six years earlier, and my ex struggled with drug addiction horribly. I had filed for divorce twice before finally leaving. Ken had been married just shy of 10 years. His ex was an addict as well; alcohol was her drug of choice. That lightning bolt stuck that late July evening, and we were inseparable. By October, we were engaged, and March 21$^{st}$ was to be our wedding. Small and intimate was the plan, just family, and we couldn't be happier.

We were just days away from our intimate wedding; all the plans were in place when a phone call changed our whole world. The local Hospital was on the line telling Ken the kids were in the backseat of their Mother's Car, involved in a head-on collision. Ken was given temporary custody of the kids at the Hospital by Child Protective Services. Their mother had been out drinking, celebrating St. Patrick's Day at the Bar with them in tow. The kids were hurt, but thank God, not too seriously.

All of a sudden, we were to be a family of five! My ex was not around at the time. His addictions took him to jail often, and when he was out, there was no way he would be alone with our son. It was hard on my son, and my other kids also had a lot going on in their minds. We tried our best to make sure they were heard, they had someone to talk to both at school and professionally, but you can't make people talk. Two years after our wedding, I became pregnant and we had a beautiful little boy. He was our glue that held our family together and we would need it. The Teens and early 20's years, it was one thing after another. We're talking serious things too.

Years passed, our birth youngest had graduated from high school and was off to college. Finally, we were to be Empty Nesters and enjoying life, when another call would come in and sweep me off my feet. I answered the phone to Child Protective Services asking me if I knew where our grandson was and his mother (our daughter). One of those "serious things" was a baby that we knew nothing about.

Our daughter had moved out of our home when she was 19 – too many rules in our home. Her birth mother had no rules. She was 24 when this adorable little boy arrived. Imagine the phone call I had to make to my husband. "Christina is pregnant." Him – "WHAT?" Then me, "and she's in labor now!" Him- "WHAT?" Talk about scrambling to find the necessities for a newborn!

It was evident that this adorable little boy had serious "issues." He couldn't suckle from a bottle correctly, and he was missing ALL of his milestone developments by months. He was almost 3 when CPS stated they felt our grandson was in grave danger. He'd been severely beaten by the boyfriend and hospitalized for five days – I picked him up, and we were asked to be his Guardian, and to say I wasn't freaking out some, I'd be lying, but he needed us. No empty nesting for us!

We adopted him that following summer, parents, again in our 50's. There were many medical appointments to follow up with. This continued as his "issues" were not getting better. At this point, his labels were; Cognitive Impaired, Severe ADHD, Dysphasia, Low Muscle Tone, Severe Developmental Delays. I'd throw in failure to thrive as he was always below the 5th Percentile of height/weight on the growth charts.

Three years passed since that dreaded phone call, and I'd had enough of the ADHD meds the Neurologist prescribed. The side effects were impeding him from functioning. My mind was made up; I'll dive into the research to get his body turned around naturally, to figure out what his body was lacking, what therapy modalities I could explore.

I'm just like you; no formal training, but I was determined! I reached out to everyone I knew in the Natural Healing World and asked questions. I read books, watched interviews of thought leaders in this movement. I changed his diet and learned specific foods are inflammatory and omitted those. I read labels on everything, and if I can't pronounce it or it has fake food coloring, it's not in the shopping cart.

I saw some small shifts in him, so I knew I was onto something. Then a dear friend said to me, "with all the research you're doing; you have to see Nutrigenomic science!" When I watched a quick video explaining Nutrigenomic science – I knew in my heart that this was something my little guy needed. I ordered the natural products, a pill made of five herbs, that have been around for centuries.

Within a few weeks, his incessant chewing stopped! His sleep improved greatly, and his words were coming through. I noticed over time; his balance was improving, the same with muscle strength. The teachers noticed a difference with him in just four months! By the end of that following school year, we would change his IEP from Cognitive Impaired Moderate to Cognitive Impaired Mild. His brain function was improving!

Fast forward to now, he is a different kid: talking in full sentences, full memory, he can dress himself totally, and he is potty trained during the day. He can play on a playground without fear that he will fall, so core strength and coordination is great. He's beginning to swim and learning to pedal. He's been learning to write and read more this year.

You may be asking yourself, can my child also shift like this? I can tell you that anything is possible with resiliency. My grandson is resilient, and he has made me resilient too!

I'd love to educate you on this amazing science of Nutrigenomics and Nutrition, and I would love to hear from you, Tina.

# Chapter Twelve

## God-Given Resilience

∽

### Dr. Venise Haynes

To single, divorced, or widowed parents who have found themselves in a duo-parenting role alone, this piece is good for you to read. Do not despair. In a blink of an eye, a divorce left me in a place to provide food, shelter, entertainment, and education to four incredible little girls.

My husband and I were high school sweethearts. He was a few years older than me. I went to his prom, and he went to my prom. In my senior year of high school, I received a scholarship to attend college. I decided to major in education. I had never been away from home, and I was enjoying meeting some incredible lifelong friends.

Meanwhile, my then-boyfriend decided to join the army. At first, I thought it was a bad decision for him, but later I understood. He tried working and obtaining support from his parents to attend college, but neither were enough, so joining the army became his final decision.

Determined to keep our relationship together, his first furlough from the army was used to come home. He arrived at the airport and then came to meet me at the bus station where I arrived from college.

When we met, it was so beautiful because we had not seen each other for several months. Unexpectedly, after we greeted each other, he kneeled down on one knee and proposed to me. I was surprised and happy, all at the same time. A crowd of people was drawn as I said yes, and the crowd began to clap.

Shortly after the marriage began, the problems began to follow. We arrived in Hanau, Germany, where he would be stationed and where we would live for the next two years. It was so far away from home; I began to miss home. From time to time, I would call my parents. However, the time and difference were so vast, waking them up made me feel at ease.

After the two-year tour in Germany was up, we were stationed in Killeen, Texas. Being in hot Texas, created a new set of problems. I often felt as if the heat made him angry, and the problem became perplexing. Fast forward, he completed his tour of duty and decided not to reenlist, so we came home and stayed with his mother, which I didn't mind because I had the most incredible mother-in-law a person could ask for, but when we came home and stayed with relatives, our marriage would soon end in divorce.

By now, I had endured many years of physical and verbal abuse and was extremely tired. Even though my resilience was beginning to take shape, I had some concerning thoughts about divorce. What would people think? What would people say? How would I tell my parents? You see, divorce in my family was not an option. However, no one knew what I was going through. It was time to put me first.

After my divorce, I came out of my comfort zone. I addressed the naysayers and decided to take complete charge of my life. My little girls needed me to take care of them. My first step was a quality home, a private school near our home, and a good babysitter.

Determined to have the best care for my daughters, I learned of a woman (stay at home mom) who lived across the street from me.

I met with her, and we established a bond immediately. Hiring her was a good decision. She knew my circumstances and embraced me and my daughters as if we were family. My daughters were all young when the divorce occurred, and my ex-husband made no attempts to have a relationship with our children or be in their lives. It was a difficult pill to swallow, but at the same time, it empowered me to become more resilient.

Time was flying. The girls were growing up fast. I needed to make more money. I took every opportunity to apply for higher-paying positions at my company; however, each position required a bachelor's degree, and I never completed college. I then made the decision to return to college to obtain my bachelor's degree, and upon completion, I secured a higher paying position. However, as the cost of living continued to rise, and my daughters' needs increased, I needed to climb that ladder to be financially secure.

By now, I was ready to return to college to obtain a doctorate degree in adult education. I completed this degree, received a promotion, and a few years later retired from that particular industry and began another career in academia. Academia was my first love, but I had put it off for marriage and work. Finally, I began teaching online and on ground.

Today, four incredible little girls are now grown women. They have strong values about education because they always saw me working and attending college. My firstborn has a master's degree in computer science and teaches online. She's married and has two children. She has been playing the piano since she was three years old. She was able to read music before she learned to read books. My second-born has a master's degree in electrical engineering. She works in that industry doing some incredible things. She is currently working on an MBA at a major university. She was the Valedictorian in grammar and high school. She received a full scholarship for her bachelor's and master's degrees. As a child, she loved to see how things worked electrically. I remember when she took our first computer completely apart. My third-born daughter is a pharmacy doctor also known as PharmD. She also carries a Master of Science in Community Health. She was a child who loved to mix up different ingredients together even if it was my good sugar or flour. She mixes medicine for cancer patients. My fourth born daughter has a master's degree in computer information and cybersecurity. She works for a major university and has two small dogs.

In conclusion, my life has been a rollercoaster. However, it has been meaningful. I learned to become bigger than my fear. I did not have a set pathway in the beginning, but it turned out to be a bridge for success for myself and my children. Always have a plan A, B, and C because you never know when things will change. Fears and trials will always come in life; however, remember to be resilient and be bigger than your fears.

# Chapter Thirteen

## *Your Journey is Your Reward*

❧

### *Kathi Holliday*

I was bewildered at a young age when I was told that "Your Journey is Your Reward." I didn't quite understand the meaning behind that saying. On graduation day, I proudly walked across the stage to receive my Associate's Degree. Very excited that I put myself through school, I was on top of the world, truly believing that I was ready to fulfill my dreams as the best computer programming analyst.

Within 3/months, I realized why the hiring companies weren't calling for interviews. They were hiring students with Bachelor Degrees, which was a serious problem since I worked part-time and attended school full time to receive my Associate Degree. My dreams had to be put on hold.

Determined to receive my Bachelor's Degree, I worked two jobs to save money for my education. I later interviewed for a permanent full-time position and I was hired on the spot. The company showed me commitment, loyalty, and stability. I felt like this was home for me. My employer also offered a tuition program, which I took advantage of to receive my bachelor's degree in business administration.

I advanced through the ranks, flourished, and successfully climbed the ladder of success. Ten ½ years later, I purchased my very 1st home, proud, excited, only to be given the devastating news 1/month after I purchased that I would be laid off (company merger). I panicked, light-headed, as I thought about my new home. Everything that I have worked for was crumbling right before my eyes. For weeks, I was alone and worried about the next journey.

Two months later, I was hired as a sales representative. I was working full time from the comfort of my home when years later, the holiday seasons were here. A week before Christmas, I slipped on a sheet of ice and down a flight of stairs, I went. To my dismay, the x-rays displayed serious ankle and shoulder damage, and unfortunately, surgery was needed.

Having a history of fatal allergic reactions, the prescriptions that the doctor gave, I choose not to take them and to just deal with the pain. Matters worsened, while recovering at home, a thrombosis formed in my right calve. For ten days, I laid in the hospital bed motionless and scared. I started thinking about the last 14 years, and tears rolled down my face, I just wanted to give up! Three weeks later, my employer informed me that I needed to start back work in two weeks. Against doctor's orders, I did, to assure that I still had my job. It didn't do me any good because months later there would be another company merger that resulted in another lay-off.

Through that experience, I've learned that it was my life that had a purpose and that should be what I focus on. Unbeknownst to me, another company heard of the layoffs and reached out to me. Back on my feet, no ankle or shoulder pain, bills paid, a new vehicle, everything was falling back into place. This perfect ride lasted only 3/ years when I received a call that I would be laid off, another merger.

For 17½ years, I've been faithful, loyal, a hard worker, and committed to three businesses that weren't to me. The definition of insanity is; I kept doing the same thing, expecting a different result. I took the time to clear my mind, read motivational, spiritual, and entrepreneurship books to build my faith. Repeating to myself that I am a winner over and over again, my confidence was back 100%. I also made up my mind about what direction to move in; I was about to take a leap towards life as an entrepreneur. I consulted a good friend. I shared my thoughts, feelings, and concerns about opening my own business. Receiving a multitude of business ideas, his encouragement and faith catapulted me to jump at the opportunity. I started investing in myself. This was exhilarating for me.

I proudly dominated the entrepreneur world for fourteen years as chief executive officer of one company and eight years with my Mobile Notary 24/7 business. My business became so successful that I realized there was no need to prospect customers anymore. My business was thriving from referrals. I was very pleased and decided to invest in myself even further as a mobile notary. I knew this was the right step towards the start of fulfilling the purpose of my journey.

After diligently learning the notary code of conduct, rules, and regulations, I became a semi-pro at witnessing signatures. In this industry, who would have thought that notaries were needed more than the research revealed. From extensive advertising and branding, my business was growing fast. Working late in the month of December, one cold, icy, snowy Chicago night, to my dismay, I had the most daunting automobile accident ever. It frightened me, so I stopped working until the winter season was over. The time taken off was utilized by packing up my belongings, advertising for rental of my home and contacting the contracting companies inquiring which (warm climate state) were notaries needed. I made a promise to myself that I would relocate before the next winter.

Relocating to Arizona in May of 2016 and changing the business name to Mobile Notary 24/7, I was blessed to successfully open within 18 (long) days of my arrival. Since my relocation, the business has been soaring and I have been enjoying the beautiful weather.

Years later, God has blessed me to meet an amazing gentleman-mentor (Mr. Gordon So), who has been an intricate part of my life since I moved here. With his help and guidance, Mobile Notary 24/7 now offers a mentorship program teaching others how to become a successful mobile notary. What Gordon has taught me is to surround yourselves with successful, like-minded people, people who are overachievers because they will lift you up and help you reach your dream. Surrounding yourself with over achievers will help you to Follow Your Dream, Never To Bargain with Life for a Penny, and always remember The Will to Win.

This is my journey and my reward and I thank you for the lessons.

# Chapter Fourteen

## Tearing Down My Castle

ᮔ

### Mike Popovici

I had enough. It seemed like all my life I'd been in some sort of fight. Fight against my perceived ignorance of the people around me, against my own thoughts constantly getting the better of me, fighting for respect, fighting for a love that always seems to demand more fighting. Everybody wants you to fight for something, but who fights for me? "Mike's got it, he'll be fine, he's on top of his game." I held onto this mindset, clinging tightly with my fist in the middle of my chest, fighting desperately to keep my life and sanity in place when it all seemed to want to tear itself apart.

I've always felt as though everyone around me will walk away and leave me for dead, or at least abandoned. As true colours come out, I wonder who is truly there for me? I would help people to the ends of the earth, where are they when I need them? Maybe they can't handle me, my gifts, my kindness, or my strengths. Or perhaps they can't appreciate my truth, my voice speaking unabated and free, and honest. Finally, open, a cry wants to pour out of my heart as I write.

My whole life, all I ever wanted is for my spirit to be free. Instead, I felt stuck in a cage that the world seemed to have built for me, a confined box I had to relegate myself to, while others played freely. Externally I was something to see; fit, young, smart, ambitious, and driven for perfection. The cage I was living in was built for me emotionally and mentally. If only I knew the mess, the stress, the structure I was functioning on was ready to crumble inside of me. Life was life; the career, the money, chasing dreams, and having them come true at every turn; built on top of a foundation made of a soul screaming to be allowed to shine. Anger at the world was bubbling inside, without me realizing it.

I always looked to others to see and know what was acceptable to say. The fighter within was fighting for recognition while drowning himself into submission out of fear of reprisal for daring to be himself. I was not able to show weakness because it was proven to be taken advantage of. Years of being bullied were my evidence. I wasn't a coward; I had no problem fighting for others. I just saw fighting creating senseless damage. For me, I could take it, so I did.

Then one day, the decision came through—if they don't understand me, if they don't appreciate the person I'm trying to be for them, if they can't get it—I'll be like them. I don't remember exactly when I made this choice, but I distinctly remember it. My heart began to close, not realizing that in making this decision, I was about to lose sight of my own light. My pain wasn't always evident to me because I carried love so naturally. Most of my life, I was the person who greeted you with a big hug and joy at you being there. You see, I was so powerfully energized and so adept at being adaptable that I couldn't realize the sadness I carried within.

My heart closing, I started succumbing to anger. My fall from grace seemed to happen silently and effortlessly, the fight to stand back up, that was a struggle I never imagined possible. Another damn fight! I was frustrated, hurt, and resentful at the world. And yet, the fighting came so naturally to me. Little did I know I was about to learn the true definition of the word. The outer fight is the easy part, and it might even get you some praise. It's the quiet inner fight that requires you to face the truth of your pain.

I remember going to my doctor to assess my constant exhaustion. He didn't need the supplements and techniques; the questions about the stress in my life said it all. In my career, I recounted how every day was a fight not to get publicly rebuked by the site leader while fighting impossible deadlines with insufficient resources." And at home?" he asked. I couldn't remember the last moment when I felt welcomed and didn't have to justify myself there as well. "I just want somewhere where I can find true peace," I said. My partner and I did our best. I needed understanding; she gave "snap out of it" love. She needed tough love; I gave too much understanding.

Divorce, perceptions of judgement, going through it all while fighting to break the pattern of why I never felt truly embraced or accepted. Surprisingly it wasn't the bullying; it was something that happened when I was much younger. To heal, I let go of the things I was doing for the wrong reasons. No more working out because I was doing it out of insecurity, I discovered. No more burning myself out in my career; enduring the letting go of that sense of self-worth. Feeling my fall from high praise, and seeing everyone shifting to speaking proudly of others that could now 'take it all on.'

Those around me were now seeing me as someone gentle, seemingly without any real fire. Getting smaller physically, being judged as not as attractive or impressive. If only they cared to know why. Never fully there, in every moment fighting back the only thing that seemed to want to come out of me-- anger. If they only knew the fire, I was fighting to suppress. I was guided now only by my soul; the only part of me that remembered my light while all I could see was dark. I embraced spirituality, even though I used to ridicule it. I sought and learned healing in ways that I only thought existed in storybooks. I felt myself standing tall in my own skin and realizing I always could have.

It was the trauma and things much deeper that clouded me. I had to go through it all to clear everything right back to my beginning. To finally embody the love I always had, boundless and full, but this time without the needing. I now fully embrace the beauty of humanity, even if others can't see it in themselves. Truly understanding compassion, love, faith, hope, forgiveness, and the freedom my soul always sought. I have a trust in myself I never knew I was missing, and an embracing of my inner warrior, jokester, lover, and teacher. I'm renewed and standing taller than I ever imagined, able to carry the world because finding my purpose took away its weight. I now embrace helping others through their beautiful journeys of personal healing and attainment. I went through what I went through so I could bring myself back to me. I'm now resilient, so I can help you find your roadmap to achieving the same.

# Chapter Fifteen

## *Focus on Faith*

∽

### *Russ Hansen*

Imagine having a successful career, beautiful home and gardens, a respected professional wife, great destinations for vacations and conferences, while living a country club lifestyle. Then one day, you wake up, and your marriage has disintegrated. A couple of your closest client friends are attacking your integrity while destroying your career. This tragedy through no fault of mine. I had enjoyed a very successful financial insurance career for almost two decades. That career included selling a personal disability policy to my former wife that paid her a tax-free income for over twenty years. Welcome to my world in late 1997. Here starts a journey of over two decades that encompasses *Resiliency For Life* personally, professionally, and physically.

My name is Russ Hansen, I am the youngest son born into a military family to Ray and Eva Hansen and have one brother Richard. I went to nine schools in thirteen years, lived in ten homes in two countries and two provinces by the time I went away to college. I had a wonderful, loving childhood with caring parents and friends still in my life over half a century later. One of the greatest gifts I ever received was the ability to stay connected with the people who have been a part of my life.

In the bestselling books, *The Road Less Travelled* by Scott Peck and *The Purpose Driven Life* by Rick Warren, they shared "Life Is Difficult" and "What on Earth am I here for?" Well, adulthood has shown me that life is indeed difficult, but how one overcomes the challenges is how we can survive and thrive. I also realize my purpose now is to bring accountability through our tragedy such that no other families should ever endure the nightmare.

In the mid-1990s, being married to a self-employed veterinarian meant you were on call 24/7 before emergency clinics became popular. The phone could ring anytime through the night and usually did. One Tuesday evening, we got a call that a cat was vomiting and was lethargic. Consulting over the phone, she prescribed a product called Laxatone for the aid of a potential hairball. Two nights later, at 10:00 p.m., the same pet owner called back that the cat was no better. My wife had them bring the cat in, and she examined the feline and found blood in the urine. The next morning x-rayed and found nothing. Decided to surgically examine the pet and found the intestines were going through necrosis, called the owner back, and asked should she continue to treat the cat or sadly euthanize? They authorized further surgery. Unfortunately, the cat didn't survive.

The distraught owner, when receiving a bill for procedures, started correspondence requesting reimbursement for pain and suffering. They further filed a complaint with the regulatory body being the College of Veterinarians in Ontario. My belief is to get out of paying their invoice. This process began the tragedy of my life. The insensitivity of the regulatory body never took into consideration the effect that they could have on a veterinarian's career, marriage, or life. Also, at that time, the Ontario Veterinary Medical Association provided no support in the matter.

While living in Southern California (2000-2013), I met Dr. Peter Weinstein DVM MBA, who presently is the executive director of the Southern California Veterinary Medical Association (SCVMA). He stated, "The practice of veterinary medicine is stressful unto itself. Working with emotional pet owners and taking care of what they feel is the most important thing in their lives takes its toll. Compound that with the stresses of running a small business and managing people and the pressure magnifies.

As a veterinarian, one thing that can truly push you to the limit is to face a complaint by the veterinary medical board or a lawsuit by a pet owner. The process of being scrutinized and put under a microscope has led to more than one (present company included) veterinarian to consider giving up being a practicing veterinarian. The impact of a board investigation goes way beyond just questioning the veterinary clinical skills and judgement. It has a deep, long-lasting, and perpetual impact on the self-confidence psyche of the veterinarian. This effect of a board's actions is rarely if ever taken into consideration. The unintended consequences of board actions may have deeper, darker results."

On the regulator's website cvo.org its banner reads *"Instilling public confidence in veterinary regulation"* and further"In serving the public interest, the College seeks to understand the risks involved in the practice of veterinary medicine and collaborates with partners to develop solutions which reduce the potential for harm to animals and people."

Dr. Bill Burbury, former president of Kingswood University in Sussex New Brunswick Canada, says, "Emotions and Feelings are neutral. Or they are not wrong. They are not to be criticized, judged, or maligned. When feelings are imposed on someone else or are translated into actions that hurt that person or someone else, then they become wrong. Every person has a right to feel any way their emotions take them. It is that simple."

While in the middle of this storm, I walked away from everything I had built, business, home, and quality of life to preserve my sanity. I had to start from scratch and moved to my native province, New Brunswick. I immersed myself in my photography and went to church while going through my grieving process. I focused on my faith to survive. I journaled weekly of what I had to be grateful for in my life.

During the next two decades, I endured many job losses and career changes while never returning to my previous economic status. In early 2008, the largest blood lab in the USA mixed up my blood and informed me that I had an incurable disease. This started a five-year professional legal nightmare.

I returned to Canada in early 2013, and in the past few years, I have gained a greater understanding of this tragedy. Through meetings with the veterinary regulatory body and correspondence with two governments, I learned valuable insight. Who regulates the regulators? No one! I hope to make a change and a difference because of this knowledge.

In late 2017, I was diagnosed with Cancer. I endured surgery and radiation. Nine months later, I survived septic shock after stopping breathing on the operating table.

This life's journey has now brought clarity. I am in the process of launching my cancer foundation **CLUB C** and my ministry *Focus on Faith*. I also married a beautiful lady in 2019 who I had known since 1998 through my church. I now know the best is yet to come on Earth as it is in Heaven.

# Chapter Sixteen

## Undercover Truth

❧

### True Bryant

I didn't know why I was glad that he was dying last summer, but now I do. There were plenty of clues along my life journey that pointed me to the truth of my childhood abuse from when I was three-years-old and of those not far from me. Every family, as Tolstoy says, has their own kind of dysfunction. And ours, like so many, revolved around secrecy, shame, and sexuality. I say this with no judgment- only compassion and a sincere desire to speak the truth.

The truth of my abuse as a little boy in Georgia came through an interesting channel. I had been visiting the Kripalu Center in Western Massachusetts 10 minutes away from my grandmother's house when I saw an advertisement for a psychic. She went by the name Alison, but that wasn't her real name. She had been a successful businesswoman in New York City for years and had begun to do psychic work because she realized she had a gift that others needed. That gift was putting individuals in touch with loved one's spirit guides and other dimensional beings that are always around us though many of us have no idea.

I was 27 when I sat down to talk with her. Bluntly, I said, "Listen, I'm excited to be here. I know something is coming up inside me. I don't know what it is. I've never been to a psychic before, so just don't give me a demon."

She laughed a little and said, "No worries. I have done this for thousands of people from all kinds of religious backgrounds, and no one has complained. I wouldn't be doing this if it didn't work."

I knew she was right. And ironically, that actually made me a little more scared. But you know what they say, "courage is not the absence of fear."

"You can contact any deceased loved ones or spirit guides and we'll just let it naturally unfold," she said.

"Well, I only have the one person I know, who is dead now, and I definitely don't love him," I said.

"Okay, no worries. We'll see what your spirit guides have to say. I need something that you have bought yourself and I need you to tell me your full birth name."

I handed her my wallet.

"Roger True Bryant II," I said.

She massaged my wallet between her smooth palms and began to say my birth name out loud, not to anyone in particular but the room. Excitement boiled within me, and for the next 25 minutes or so, there was a presence in the room of my spirit guide. I never saw it with my physical eyes, but I certainly felt it. Some of you reading may think that is simply delusional, but those who have tried this will know what I'm talking about.

At around the 30-minute mark, something shifted.

"Ugh," I said, my hand on my stomach. I was doubled over in my chair. Whatever it was about to be revealed to me. And it wasn't pleasant.

"I see myself as a baby. Weak, innocent, unstained by the world," I muttered. "I'm at my house in Norcross, Georgia. My parents and sisters aren't at home. He is there, though. Ugh."

I stayed doubled over in my chair, rubbing my belly and scrunching my mouth up in disgust while looking at the floor. Alison stayed present across the table. It wasn't her first rodeo.

"Did he abuse me sexually? I need you to ask my spirit guide," I loudly whispered to Alison.

"Okay, one moment."

She closed her eyes for a few beats.

"They say, yes, that is correct."

I moaned deeply, partly to release anger and slightly to allow this truth to sit in the space.

It had been such a long time coming. I had always sensed it. Someone close to me talked about how he had done things to her that no man should. He had a presence about him that drew certain women like honey. People often said, "if you could sell that kind of charisma, we'd be wealthy." Unfortunately, "charisma" can take someone to dark places, abusive behaviors, and tragic selfishness.

I looked at Alison and asked, "can you ask my Guides how many times he did this to me?"

She closed her eyes again. I felt queasy, raging, and profoundly betrayed. But I also felt relieved that this under-the-surface intuition had finally been validated, physically, and emotionally with someone else in the room. I wanted to make sure.

"How do I know this is true and that these spirits aren't just fucking with me?"

She closed her eyes.

"They're saying; there's no reason for us to lie. We're just confirming your suspicions."

I nodded. I knew they were right.

I jerked up my head and stared at Alison.

"Whoa, it's wild that the one person that I didn't want to deal with was him, and yet that's where the true knowledge was..."

She looked at me. "Stand up." I stood, somewhat reluctantly. She grabbed me gently on both shoulders and looked right up at me.

"Listen to me. These things happen. You're not alone. I want you to know that you're a beautiful man and that this does not define you. It's only shaped you. And you can use this knowledge to support others and speak boldly about what you've overcome. How you've experienced this type of abuse from relatives and have decided to rise above it."

I wiped the tears from my face.

"Ground yourself, learn to forgive him, and decide right now not to let this distort your future. Do you hear what I'm saying?"

I was out of it, but listening to every word.

"Yeah. I get it. I know what I need to do."

So here I am, writing, speaking, serving others as a private coach of high-level professionals. I know that under nice suits and public awards can lay terrifying shame and brokenness.

I am called to witness this in my fellow humans. I am called to hold sacred space for men (and women) so that they may be seen, heard, witnessed.

I am dedicated to causes that expose this type of shameful, destructive behavior to children.

Through it all, I've decided to take Susan's advice. I will not be defined by this evil.

I choose to stand up.

I choose to speak up.

I choose resilience.

# Chapter Seventeen

## *Resiliency, Embrace the Possible*

⤬

### *Susy Giddy*

*Dedication: To my baby brother Chris, whose death taught
me to live; to my dear sisters Becky and Jenny without whom
I could not travel this journey of grief; and to the great love of
my life, my husband Martin, whose love has healed my heart, I
dedicate this story of loss, hope, and love.*

One thing I know for sure, as Oprah would say, it is not what happens
in your life, it is how you choose to respond, that determines the
impact that the circumstances will have on your life. You might be
thinking at this moment: What if it is something horrific? I know
about horrific! When I was 17-years-old, the most unthinkable of
the many unthinkable events of my life took place on a Saturday in
January. A day that started out like any other Saturday would change
my life and the lives of the rest of my family forever.

After arguing over morning chores, I zipped off to the local mall, more
of a leisure activity with girlfriends, rather than a shopping expedition.
A couple of hours later, I returned home and saw the minister walking

down the path in front of my parent's house. "What happened? Is it my father? Is it my mother?" "No," said the grim and paled face minister, "it is Chris, he is dead" This would be the beginning of a whirling, incredibility, that would last for many years, and maybe does even to this day, as I tried to comprehend the unthinkable.

How could my adorable, pesky full of life little brother be D-E-A-D? Then came the horrifying explanation, he accidentally died of autoerotic asphyxiation. In other words, while self-pleasuring, just at the moment of sexual climax, he tightened a belt around his neck and died. The intention is to amplify the experience, not to die.

A practice that takes the lives of many young people each year. At the time, I had never heard of it, and in a pre-Google world, information was hard to come by. We did not talk about how he died. I did not understand what happened, only that he was found hanging in his closet by our Mother. Imagine trying to understand an accidental hanging with the additional layer of the sexual context. It was pretty much too horrible, too confusing to grasp. What I know is that he got the idea from a magazine. I also know that all these years later, these kinds of tragic accidents still occur. It happens because we don't know about it or talk about it. So, we can't warn our youngsters and often don't know how to comfort families of the accident victims.

And so began, my experience learning to cope with the unthinkable. It was the days of Elizabeth Kubler Ross "On Death and Dying" and Harold Kushner, "When Bad Things Happen to Good People," Books that I read cover to cover, over and over to try to understand, to cope with the grief and to make sense of the senseless loss. I tried to go in an orderly fashion through the stages of grief: denial, anger, acceptance, and so on, but grief is not orderly and obedient, as we now know.

Through this loss, my journey was and has been without a map, but more with a guide that comes from inside me. I call the guide love; it started with the love of my little brother; it grew to a love of life and the greatest understanding of how precious it is. My love grew to include the good fortune of marrying the love of my life and raising wonderful children. It includes the magnificent love for my only grandchild, Max! I have chosen to live in places I love like a Caribbean Island and to do the things I love, like skiing, dancing, and being with my dog, Ruffus. It is as though the only way to heal a broken heart is to love and be loved as much as one possibly can. It is a journey that never ends. As the anniversary of my brother's death arrives, I celebrate his life by finally telling this story. I hope that it helps prevent further accidental deaths.

Our son, Robin, lived with a deadly form of brain cancer for 17 years, and during the solar eclipse of the sun on August 21st, 2017, he died. His ashes lie at the Summit of Mont Tremblant, and each day of the ski season, we ski by the spot, greeting him each morning and bidding him goodnight each evening. Sometimes we ski while crying for his loss, and sometimes we ski while talking to him and asking questions. We also survived what should have been a fatal accident. Martin while driving, fainted in my arms, the car careened down the highway, rolled completely over and popped up breaking Martin's neck, as we were rolling over and I thought my life was ending, I understood a great truth. When we come to the end of our lives, all that matters is how well we loved, how well we gave and received love.

When I understand the most important principle of my form of Resiliency, it is to truly embrace the possible; whether that is to know we can survive and thrive no matter what comes our way or to achieve any dream, it begins with embracing the possible.

My brother had a short and sweet life, his death was a tragedy, but in his death lies the gift of life. I learned, as Dr. Edith Eva Eger, a survivor of Auschwitz, and one of my heroes, says, to Embrace the Possible. To choose how to live with each circumstance that comes my way, whether that be to grieve for loss and still find love or to discover the joy in any adventure. For that gift, I will be eternally grateful to my baby brother, Christian John Rees Ruedy, June 22, 1957- January 15, 1972. It is my hope with all my heart that this story gives hope and love where they are most needed.

# Chapter Eighteen

## The Dream

❧

### Darrel Howell

They say that in most families, the youngest child is spoiled, well, that was not the case for me. If anything, it was the opposite. As a young kid growing up on Chicago's south side with two older siblings, my goals and endeavors seemed to be predetermined by my parents. If there was something my brother or sister was successful at, I was also expected to be successful at those things. That made it tough for me because I've always been my own man. I didn't believe in following a guideline as if I was programmed.

During my years of grammar school and high school, I did what I needed to get by. I wanted to be in the spotlight, an athlete, an actor, or a singer, something in the entertainment field, and as far as I knew, you didn't need an education for that.

As I matured in my years at school, I never lost sight of what I wanted to be. In my household, no one supported me to pursue my dreams; it was just a pipe dream that I would never be able to reach, so I just continued on with my education.

While attending college, I was studying hard, reading, writing, and taking classes to get a degree, but while doing this, I still had in the back my mind to entertain. I thought maybe I'll have to do it teaching in a classroom. That would be my audience.

I also auditioned for a radio station and was instantly hired, which allowed me to find myself. As the years went by, I started hearing different music and new lyrics in my mind. I soon found out I had a friend who had a four-track recording studio, and he said I was welcome to come and record. I was loving every minute, and I wanted to continue no matter what.

I continued to grow, and as I did, I needed musical instruments and a larger recording source. I bought a new keyboard and my own recording studio so that I could work on my music at any time. All of this was in the late 1980s, which made me unable to be heard on a larger plateau because social media was nonexistent, so I began saving my money to move to Los Angeles, California.

My mother began to notice the determination, and she said to me, "You have a cousin who lives in L.A., I'll give him a call." He welcomed me to stay with him. I loaded up that car with so much stuff I could barely see out the windows. Oh, was I ever nervous, it was just me, my music, and the road in front of me.

I got about as far as St. Louis, Missouri; I got a hotel room for the night. After getting settled in my hotel room I decided to go and get something to eat while heading to a restaurant, I ran into a college friend who was also a musician, and he was telling me that he was touring with the artist, STING. We talked for a few minutes, but I was on a mission, so I kept it short and sweet. I slept the nervousness off and got back on the road. Within an hour of driving on the road, a rainstorm hit with lightning and thunder. I had to lower the speed of my car just to be able to still see the road. My windshield wipers weren't wiping fast enough to get a good vision of where I was going, and it was getting dark, but I was to determine not to stop, so I drove into the night until the sun began to rise again.

In Oklahoma, I looked and saw what appeared to be a tornado. It looked like something out of a movie. Then over the radio, they confirmed a tornado was coming my way. There was nothing but country all around me, and there was a tornado heading right towards me in the middle of the road. When it got so close, I pulled over, and then about five minutes later, the tornado hit my car. I think because I had so much stuff in it that it didn't turn over, but at least two or three times it raised up on two wheels, and I am praying that I would survive, but just as quick as it hit me, it left. I was in shock from that event and began to wonder if I was doing the right thing, but I had come too far to turn around. Cell phones weren't the norm at that time, so there was no one to call.

I decided to call it a night in New Mexico City, and when I woke up in the morning and got back on the road, I got word that a hurricane was brewing in New Mexico. Here we go again, I thought to myself. As I continued down the road, I could see a dark gray wall in front of me. I drove right into it. I could barely see in front of me; the wind was blowing my car from side to side. I figured if I could hold steady, I could drive through it, and in about an hour, I did. From there on, the sun was shining, the wind was calm, and everything looked bright. Before I knew it, I was arriving in Los Angeles, and it was time for me to live out my dream.

While I was at my cousins, I was downstairs talking and asked to use the bathroom, it was being occupied, so I went to the upstairs one, not knowing that I was about to reach a turning point in my life. I overheard my two cousins having a discussion about me; they had no idea I was there. My female cousin was saying, "I know he wants to do music and came out here to live, but I don't think he has what it takes to make it." My male cousin said, "You know I talked to him for about a year off and on and he seems very focused, and I believe in him, and if you don't want him to stay with you then I will let him stay with me and sleep on my couch because I think he's gonna make it." When I heard those words, what it did to my heart and soul meant everything to me. Finally! Someone believes in me. I knew that what he was saying was honest and pure because he did not know I was listening, nor did she. Upon hearing that, I think I became even more resilient in my quest to succeed.

I eventually got a job that allowed me to write songs and put together the music to go along with the lyrics. I started to recruit singers and would enter them into talent shows. While at a club in L.A., I ran into a female friend who had started a rap group and had been signed to a contract with Eazy-E, the founder of N.W.A. They needed eight more songs and only had two days to get it done. It was right up my alley because I had at least 30 songs in my library that they could use. I had to sign a contract as a ghost producer and writer (for those who don't understand, it means that I get paid for producing and writing the lyrics, but my name does not go on the album, it would be credited to Eazy-E). It was my first gig; I didn't care. So, I did it! From there, I composed a few songs for Anita Baker, Whitney Houston, The Whispers, Babyface, and a group called the Deele.

As time moved on, I got married, and things slowed down. I got divorced, and it slowed things down even more. I had children and got married again, but I choose to remain resilient because that's what I do. And I'll always choose to chase my dreams!

# Chapter Nineteen

## The First Step To A New Life

❧

### Andrew Alberlan

*"Out of suffering have emerged the strongest souls,*
*the most massive characters are seared with scars"*
*—Kahlil Gibran*

It is said that a 1,000-mile journey begins with a single step, sometimes it would appear that we are unaware at the time, we are taking that first step on a journey that will forever change our lives.

I trace my thoughts back to spring 2015; my neighbour was getting materials delivered to construct a hopyard, to grow hops for brewing beer. The hopyard would consist of about 2 acres of land that needed 100 telephone poles, 30 feet in length to be stood up, and inserted in the ground to form the supports for the trellis wire that the future hop vines would climb. For this, we rented a telehandler, which is a large tractor with an arm that can extend, at the end of the arm are forks, like a forklift.

We worked for a week straight, through heat, rain, mechanical issues, and exhaustion. Finally, the last pole had been set. My neighbours father, who had been running the telehandler for most of the project, fired up the telehandler to put it away. I turned to walk away from the machine as he began to back up. As I did, the articulated body of the machine, which is how it steers, pivoted towards me and I felt the 5-foot tall tractor tire grab the heel of my boot. In an instant, I was dragged to the ground as the machine proceeded to run its way up my left leg. It seemed to go in slow motion; I could feel the crushing weight of the 20,000 lb machine grinding my foot and ankle into the ground.

The initial x-rays revealed only one broken toe, a plaster splint was formed to my foot, and I was sent home with crutches. I was in good spirits and determined to do my best to get on with life. I was scheduled to see an orthopedic surgeon, ten days after the incident. He told me that after an in-depth CAT scan, there was more damage than previously thought, he suggested installing a plate and stainless steel screws to support the joint.

I was informed that if I did not have the surgery, I would never walk again without pain, if it ever really healed at all. To say that I was devastated by this prognosis is an understatement, on the drive home, I reflected on my conversation with the surgeon, the idea of installing metal in my foot did not sit well with me. Questions and concerns flooded my mind; I foresaw a life of potential issues with this game plan.

I was inspired at that moment to heal myself. The following week I went back to the surgeon and informed them I would be opting out of the surgery. I became very solid within myself that I alone was the expert of my body, that I alone was responsible for my body, and that it would heal itself if I would just allow it to do so.

From the moment the decision was made to trust my instincts and promote my own healing, it had become very apparent that I needed some help. My emotions had been a roller coaster. I was also aware that there was the possibility of energy blockages in my body that could inhibit the healing process. So along with a large daily dose of vitamins and minerals, I enlisted the help of an energetic healer to release trapped emotions and balance my energy fields to further promote efficient healing.

In late July, I walked into the doctor's office, in my sneakers, unassisted. No crutches, no boot. Astonished, the doctor asked me to walk from one end of the office to the other, pivot, then walk back. It was slow and deliberate, but I performed the task. It had been just over two months since that fateful day.

I did continue to heal and gain strength. I continued to recover emotionally, physically, and mentally. Over the next few months, I recovered my physical strength so I could get back to work and start rolling back the financial tide. Some weaknesses in my marriage had been revealed during this ordeal. There was constant stress in the background; in the coming years, it would unravel and end in divorce.

Slowly I began to recover financially and to grow as a person, for the first time truly perceiving that there was something larger for me to be done with this life than I had previously been aware of. Five years later, my life has changed drastically. I have a new amazing relationship with a woman that exceeds my wildest dreams. I am physically and mentally a stronger person than I was, due to having endured the healing process and making that mindset of improvement a part of my regular life. This experience, which I previously viewed as one of my most tragic moments, actually has come to be known to me as one of my life's most powerful gifts.

When that pinnacle moment shows up, one that causes you to define your life as before and after, as it did with me, embrace it, feel grateful for it, for at that moment, our lives will never again be the same and that is a beautiful blessing. Further proof that when we view each experience as a blessing or a lesson, which is a gift, given to us for the purpose of transforming us into the person that we are today so that we can then be the person that the world needs us to be tomorrow. I look forward with excitement, enthusiasm, and expectancy to a world where we can all become aware of our greatest gifts and strengths, to build a better future for us all. Thank you, and God bless.

# Chapter Twenty

## *Learning to Love Me*

∞

### *Jennifer Doyle*

I'm truly blessed to be influenced and nurtured by loving parents who are always there for me. They are strong people who have made an amazing life for their five children, me being the youngest. Having such love and security in my home life, allowed me to have wondrous experiences out in the world as a young person to adulthood.

We encounter many things along our path, whether they come from our day to day or outside sources, such as people who are kind or mean or others who call you names or bully. These create emotions that instill fears within us or they create strengths that uplift and inspire us.

There are so many things that can happen to us along the way that leads us to how we feel about our looks or our bodies and the actions we take in life. Whether we are born with or developed these thoughts and feelings, they impact us by way of how we see ourselves.

They mold us and affect either part of our subconscious or buried emotions. Sometimes, these feelings can fuel our everyday decision making or the decisions we fail to make. We are what we think and live the life we feel worthy of, with what we have and what we know and understand. The power of thinking and feeling drives the direction in where we go.

From the earliest stages of my memory, I always felt confused by so many things about myself. Perhaps this is normal for everyone, but I certainly remember how all-encompassing it was and that it was with me all the time as a young person. I also thought I was the only one feeling what I did and I think that is why I never spoke about it or shared it before. I did not feel that I was attractive. I did not feel ugly by any means but I always compared myself to others.

The impact of it really hits me hardest now when I think about it because when I look back to those confusing years and how I felt inside, how much I wished so hard that I could be like other girls, thinking that that would make my life better and how I was so hard done by that they were given the great body and looks but I wasn't. I remember asking God why? I understand so much more now but back then it was real and I had no idea what to do with it.

When I look back at photographs of myself, knowing how I felt, I'm shocked and surprised that I felt the way that I did. I see now that I was beautiful and that my body was too! You could have complimented me back then, but I would not have absorbed that as true. I was not ready to see it or hear it. I needed to learn more about what was important in life and what was important to me and go through my process.

I grew and learned and moved forward as we do. I put all my love, heart, and soul into being a wife, mother, and career woman. I learned how to play guitar and became a singer-songwriter and love being creative. I was also blessed with true love and amazing kids. I love every minute of it. Being the best I could be, making sure everyone was well cared for and let everyone feel my care and passion. This fueled me and made me feel good inside. It was what I was really good at, taking care of others. But there was something missing within me that I did not see for so many years. I had forgotten about ME!

Whether subconscious or not, it had been much easier for me to take care of others than to take care of myself. I had been feeling robotic, with no motivation or inspiration. I felt that I had so much more to achieve within myself and could be more than a wife and a mom. I was doing a job that I enjoyed but wanted more.

So, I began to plug into many kinds of personal development, met incredible people, and challenged myself and my fears. I began an entrepreneurial project which stimulated me. It gave me a challenge to better myself. To do things I have never done before. I was feeling the fear and doing it anyway and I felt great! I took different courses and read amazing books that I never thought of reading before. I had dreams that I thought were unattainable, that I now know I will attain.

I do not regret one moment of what has made me today. I have learned so much about how the universe works, how it flows and how I am the one directing it and I can choose to keep being stuck or allow myself to soar and lead my life to be or become whatever I want. I know that now, I feel it in my soul so strong I am shouting it from the rooftops, "Look out world, here I come!"

In challenging myself to grow and learn new things, I built my confidence and amazing things started to happen. I feel the excitement and have the vision for things I never imagined because I had never imagined it was reachable. I expanded myself and want to inspire others to do the same. I can do anything if I believe. I understand the proverbial magical key was me, loving myself, connecting with myself, looking within the hidden corridors, and opening the doors to tap into the dormant parts of myself, awakening and setting myself free of any limitations.

I'm now following my heart and creating my future. I feel strong and steady on my path that nothing will deter me. I love myself unconditionally, and I'm loved by others. I'm not alone in my journey, and I know that now. I have been created for a reason, and I am so proud of my accomplishments and am very excited about the legacy and imprint I will leave for my family and on this world to make it a better place.

# Chapter Twenty-One

## *Live4Life Now*

&infin;

### *Robert Lawrence*

There were three life-shattering moments when I felt like the world's weight suddenly collapsed on my entire body, and my new reality became obscured, numb, and painful. They were the darkest moments in my life, and I felt completely hopeless with a monumental void. It was April 2010 when I was diagnosed with Stage 2—Hodgkin's Lymphoma cancer at 35-years-old and then again in October 2015 and that time leading to a stem cell transplant scheduled in January 2016. It was entirely foreign and new to me since no one ever had cancer in my immediate family. It was devastating for me to receive the news, and I felt completely vulnerable, angry, alone, sad, and lost. It was like I had just received my death sentence on a megaphone from the Doctor—you have cancer!

I immediately started asking myself, "What did I do wrong in life to deserve this cancer?" Is this something that I had brought on to myself? I had a thousand questions but didn't even know where to begin. The anger in me raged like fire because I wasn't ready to succumb to chemotherapy and let it deteriorate my body and physical appearance. I feared the painful needles, the pricking, the vomiting, muscle pains, hair loss, and the uncontrollable mood swings that came with the chemo and other drugs. I could either fight it or surrender to it, and that's when I knew that I wanted to live and fight for life!

One thing I could do and still had control of was my mind. I could let this rotten disease consume me or I could consume it—out of existence. Yes, I knew that I would have to endure the needles, the surgeries, the physical pain and all the other intolerable side effects that came with chemo, but after realizing that I was not ready to die—I started my own mental battle, and that's when I chose to *Live4Life Now.*

I found myself lying on the hospital beds trembling with fear, vomiting, and sweating from anxiety, but then I told myself, "Robert, you are going to win this battle and you are not going to accept it." Of course, I knew that there would be painful, depressing, and sad days ahead, but this is the journey that I was chosen for, and I put my trust into God and the universe. I somehow accepted that the journey was far bigger than me and it was something I couldn't immediately understand. I knew that this would help me inspire, motivate, and empower others in their battles with cancer.

Each time that I did chemotherapy, I found myself mentally 'checking out' to a place that I could find serenity and absence of pain. I would transfer and diffuse my entire spiritual energy and being to the white sands of Maui, Hawaii. I just listened to the waves, feeling the trade winds against my body and the mist of the water wash upon my face, as I mentally meditated to a place of pleasure. I considered these moments my most awakening because it was there that I felt completely alive and connected to my spirit. I profoundly meditated while in the hospital bed, as I was being poked, pricked, and infused with the toxic chemicals that made me physically weak and sick. I consistently told myself that I did not have cancer, although, I could feel it consuming my entire body. I began to empower myself with motivation, positive thinking and absorbed miraculous energy and power that seemed to come from another dimension. Wherever it came from, I decided that I was going to harness it for my battle to survive.

I chose to speak and yell at every cancer cell that imbibed my body and commanded, "I am more powerful than you, and you will not have me or my body!" I did this every day, even while I was at home. I believed that by saying those powerful words, that I would somehow eliminate and manifest that disease out of existence. It was an internal battle, and the struggle was all too real because I would silently cry like I was fighting an unknown and invisible enemy.

Though there were difficult days when I felt hopeless, fatigue, and sick—I never gave up. I never surrendered to the disease and visualized myself being cured. I created my very own internal vision board, which consisted of many beautiful things: family, friends, holiday celebrations, joyful events, the births of nieces and nephews, but most importantly, I saw myself living in an abundant world free of cancer and free of pain. I was able to manifest my way back to the freedom of life by visualizing the life that I so desperately wanted to hold on to; this happened not once, not twice, but three times in my life.

After the physical and mental battles with endless surgeries, I would miraculously open my eyes each and every time and said, "Wow, Robert, you are a warrior, a survivor, a fighter, and you are definitely here for a reason bigger than yourself." The reason is to share my story, so I can help inspire, motivate, and empower others. I had to overcome the darkness, the mental battles, the lonely tears, the depression, and fight for life. Though the journey was long, dark, painful, and lonely at times, I chose to fight for my life and surrender to the power of my mind. I became resilient to anything that was thrown at me and knew that I only had two options: choose to live for life now or let the invisible toxic enemy consume me with no mercy and destroy my being out of existence. I am resilient, I am powerful and I am a leader who can help you fight your battle and choose to live for life—now.

# Chapter Twenty-Two

## *My Greatest Gift*

∞

### *Kelly (McDermott) Chiasson*

Imagine *receiving* the *greatest gift* in the entire world and I mean really imagine it. A special something that you'd dreamt about *your* whole life.

Now, imagine *gifting* the *greatest gift* in the entire world. A special something someone else had dreamt about *their* whole life.

Let's go back in time a little bit. I grew up in Omaha, Nebraska. I was just 22-years-old and I knew all about gratitude, grace, blessings, and selflessness. What I didn't know was that I was going to be called to embody these with all my strength and heart.

As a kid, I always wanted to be a mom when I grew up. And to me that meant being married with a husband, having a bunch of kids, creating memories, having fun, and doing big things (as I always had massive visions for my future). I loved growing up in my home. My family was the BEST! I loved my mom, dad, siblings, and extended relations! Growing up, family time was the priority. Oh the memories! Whether it was our home life, game nights, birthdays, special occasions, vacations, road trips, family gatherings, cousin get-togethers, talent shows, or overnights at Gram's... year after year we just created so many memories! THIS was what life was all about! My parents had set the stage; they loved each other and they loved us. This is what I wanted in my adult life; more of what I grew up with. That was my plan.

Life however, had bigger plans in store for me. In my heart, I believe we all have the strength and capacity to handle life's experiences. In February 1998, I found out that I was several months pregnant. Wow, a baby! Life's greatest gift and yet my heart sank because I hadn't forgotten my dream and the instant reality of a choice I had made conflicted with how I wanted to raise my future children. Families come in all shapes, sizes, colors, genders, and cultures. I love them all! For me though, I knew this baby had to have a mom and a dad and the same opportunities I had. Keeping the baby just because I wanted to be a mom, wasn't a good enough reason for me. Keeping my baby would have been for selfish reasons and that's when I knew my gift was intended to be someone else's gift.

As time went on, I discovered I was having a boy! He would be 'on loan' to grow until it was his time to go. It's a unique feeling to carry around a gift for nine months. I put some meaningful family names to use and named him James Paul so I could bond with him throughout my pregnancy. I absolutely loved being pregnant and I loved him!

Opportunities, blessings; they surround us. It's in acknowledging them and sitting with them that we grow in strength, character, grace and gratitude. I grew in more ways than one over the remainder of my pregnancy.

I would regularly talk to James Paul about his family (that I had yet to find) and asked the guy upstairs to assist in my search. There's a saying that says, "we receive what we put out." Well, I received exactly what I put out. The next greatest gift that I had received came a few months later, in the number of three, and they are my living angels. They would end up being my birth son's Mom, Dad, and big brother!

Remember back when I was filling you in on the whole family thing I had planned for myself? Guess what? They had ALL of that! I loved them the moment I met them! I loved them and they loved me right back. Their son was nine at the time and they had been trying to add to their family for seven years. We were meant to meet. You see, my gift was their gift all along. It's just that their son had to stop by my tummy to get to know me and my family on his way to meet them.

I love this family more than they'll ever know. I love my birth son more than he'll ever know. I love that I had an entire week to bond with him and introduce him to all of my family before going home to his family. I love that his big brother got to name him. They kept James as his middle name so he would carry me, his birth mom with him throughout his life. Our families know each other, he shares his birthday with my husband, he was our ring bearer, they were in our wedding, and we have a relationship to date! He has had and will always have all the love and opportunities he deserves. I love that we are in each other's lives. And I love that I had the privilege of giving the greatest gift in the entire world.

All those years ago, I sat in grace and gratitude, believing that his family would 'show up.' And they did. I also wondered what the opportunity would look like for me to share my story one day. I decided I would reside in grace and gratitude once again, and trust that it too would 'show up.' And twenty-two years later, it did. Here I am, co-authoring a book with my birth son's mom! You'll get to read her story next.

Over the years, I have had my own opportunity to have all that 'family stuff' I always wanted! My husband and I are raising 4 incredible kids, creating memories, having fun, and loving every minute of it!

You know, I always had an amazing imagination, and yet I never could have imagined just how great my greatest gift would ever be. Dallas James, my world became a better place because you came into it!

22.22.22 for you and me, D.

# Chapter Twenty-Three

## *My Treasured Gift*

$\infty$

### *Theresa Cole*

Twenty-two years ago, we received a beautiful gift from one incredible woman named Kelly. Dallas was born into the world, with so much love surrounding him. His birth-mom was there to see him open his eyes for the first time, as his mom and dad waited to take him to his new loving home. Our hearts were filled with so much joy throughout the adoption process; I still remember it like it was yesterday.

When Kelly called to say she had chosen us, we were over the moon. After nine years of secondary infertility, we were going to have a baby boy! Kelly said her most favorite thing to do was to give presents, and she didn't know of a better present she could give than her baby boy. We would have an open adoption, so she would now be a part of our extended family.

After we celebrated the birth of Dallas with Kelly and her family, we brought home our beautiful dark-haired, brown-eyed baby boy. Between my husband Kevin, our nine-year-old son, Austin, and myself, he had no choice but to get spoiled. We couldn't get enough of him. Austin was so excited to finally have a sibling. Dallas wasn't much of a sleeper, but Kevin and I took turns getting up with him, so one of us could always get some sleep. Knowing he was our last child made it easy to get up. I cherished every moment I got to snuggle with him.

Dallas was a healthy baby, always at the top of the charts for weight and height. I always said he was the most beautiful baby I ever saw! He was a little late with milestones, like crawling and walking, but nothing too out of the ordinary. It was no big deal from our standpoint, until 18-months-old when Dallas began to have tantrums. At first, we thought, oh, he's just hitting the terrible two's a little early, but his speech was also delayed, and he would get very easily frustrated. If he wanted something, and you couldn't figure out what he wanted, a tantrum would occur. They could last over an hour, and there was no consoling him. He would scream until he was so tired he would just fall asleep.

When it was time for the daycare years, Dallas began to manipulate the other kids and teachers to have things the way he wanted them. No one could sit in his spot. No one could play with the toys he liked. If they did, they probably got knocked down, bit, or had the toy thrown at them. We were getting more and more complaints from the staff. We were always reading parenting books and asking for ideas from them on solutions, but the response we received was that we didn't know how to discipline our child.

Dallas liked things 'his way.' When we read him books, he wouldn't let us stop, or he would have a meltdown. His bedroom was full of Teddy Bears and Matchbox cars. At night, we would have to turn every bear around because "they were looking at him," and the cars would have to be parked perfectly in lines. One of us would have to stay in his room with him, and even then, he wouldn't go to sleep.

A friend referred us to see a doctor that specializes in behavior disorders. That was the beginning of our medical journey. By completing a lot of questionnaires and tests with the behavioral doctor, Dallas was diagnosed with ADHD and ODD. He was extremely smart, but because he could be non-compliant, it didn't always look that way on paper. We didn't want to medicate him if at all possible, so the doctor suggested a Child Psychologist, who could help us work with Dallas on his anger and sleeping issues. To get him to sleep, the Psychologist suggested we turn the lock around to the outside on his bedroom door and let him cry it out. It was torture for us to listen to him cry. He would cry for over an hour and destroy his room. I can't tell you how many holes were in his door and walls from Matchbox cars or anything he could find to throw. If you took them away, he would just find something else to destroy.

In elementary school, we were very involved in his day-to-day schooling by communicating with his teachers. Every teacher that worked with him loved Dallas because he was a lovable child when he was happy. Unfortunately, he was getting consequences in the "safe room" more and more, which meant when they couldn't settle him down, they would put him in an isolated area, shut and lock the door so that he could work through his tantrum. When I would pick him up from school, he would be absolutely exhausted. It was just heartbreaking.

At the end of second grade, Dallas ran away from me at a school carnival. When I found him, I had to put him in a hold and carry him to the car while he was screaming and kicking. In the car, he unbuckled his car seat and jumped out of the van when I began to drive down the road. It had gotten to the point that we were so afraid. Our friends had seen Dallas's struggles first hand and referred us to the Boys Town Inpatient Residential Treatment Center for more intensive therapy. There was a lot of crying involved in making the decision. It was traumatic for both him and us to leave him at the center. For the next 18 months, we were only allowed to talk to him on the phone 10 minutes per day and visit him for one hour on the weekends if he earned it.

Halfway into 4th Grade, Dallas was released, and we had learned through weekly therapy how to work through behavioral issues. Now that he was home, it was imperative to stick to the program and not give in to any manipulation. They started integrating him into the regular classroom, little by little until by the end of the school year he was mainstreamed.

In middle school, his class clown phase came out. The good news was he was so smart, and his grades were very good. His math teacher said he could be genius-level if he put his mind to it. He loved competing in sports, and throughout all of junior high, he never had an aggressive incident, which was fantastic!

When it was time for high school, we had moved school districts, so most of his friends were not in this school system. Dallas didn't want anyone to know about his behavior disorder, so if he needed to meet with his school psychologist, he would sneak into her office when no one would see him. It was difficult for him to focus on lecture-style learning in high school, so he was struggling a bit. Finding outlets in sports helped him evolve. He came home one day and said he was trying out for golf. He hadn't played much before, so we didn't expect he would make the team. But when Dallas puts his mind to it, he would make it happen. Not only did he make the team, he even went to state golf his senior year. He also went to Administration for approval to start a fishing team. I was very proud. To this day, fishing is his greatest love.

Dallas is now 22-years-old and living on his own. He's enrolled in Full Sail University in an online program for Video Gaming and Design and working part-time at a retail golf store. He has not had any aggressive behavior issues since grade school and has the tools he needs to stay focused. My son is a happy, loving, smart, and energetic person that can truly accomplish anything he sets his mind to. Thank you, Kelly, for this treasured gift.

# Chapter Twenty-Four

## Resiliency By Law

∽

### Samantha F. Glass

Life is a gift that we don't often see at first as we navigate our way through the unknown. Maybe it's because we don't know how to use what we are given to its fullest potential. I have faced many obstacles throughout my life's journey, ones that I found myself trying to run from, instead of facing them head-on. Sometimes, fear takes ahold of you and challenges you to not let emotions control your life.

In business, we face the pressures of those that are jealous and try to tear us down. Imagine being someone with low confidence and you are trying to work your way towards being a success. It takes persistence and ambition to ensure that those outside influences don't affect us. Once you are able to drown out the outside noise, the ability to create becomes easier.

There is no manual to life telling us that we need basic accounting skills, money management, what to eat, how to exercise, etc. What there is, is a flood of information that we need to decipher. We need to push ourselves to try multiple things to see what works. It's not a simple task, but it's necessary in order to succeed. Things in life can seem that they are not working in our favor. It's not so much that the methods we are using aren't working, but rather that we haven't given them enough time to bear fruit. Have patience and persistence and never give up!

I started my paralegal practice years ago, as I saw a gap in the legal system. There are those individuals that could obtain legal aid and those that could afford lawyers, however, there was no one to help the everyday person. Individuals and businesses were expected to represent themselves. This caused a backup in the court system as those that went on their own often clogged the system as they were not trained. **I AM THE SOLUTION!** My persistence over the years, however, has helped me on my path to grow the largest paralegal firm in Ontario. My passion for the law and seeing the way I change my client's lives for the better is the fuel that drives my passion in my practice.

**I am not only Resilient for myself, but I am Resilient for others!**

One of the most challenging obstacles I face in my career is that most people are still unclear about how my profession can assist them. Social media stereotypes portray paralegals as law clerks or legal assistants that require supervision by lawyers. In most countries, this is true, with Ontario, Canada being the exception.

Here's why: in Ontario, Canada – paralegals are regulated and licensed by The Law Society of Ontario to provide legal services similar to that of a lawyer, within a defined scope of practice. We are independent and do not need to practice under the supervision of a lawyer, although some may choose to. My firm is a litigation firm and is often representing clients in court on various matters independent of lawyers.

Facing personal challenges in life and then assisting others with their challenges takes strength and power. It takes care and understanding and the ability to be a fierce advocate to bring justice to those who are unable to stand up for themselves. Over the years, I have taken the time to learn about myself and discover the powers inside of me. I now possess superpowers I could have never imagined!

We often negate who we are to assist others because we want to help; however, this does no justice as we are not at full strength. Learning about myself and how to face challenges better has equipped me to be the best version of myself and to be that strength that others need from me as an advocate.

I am the voice for those that do not have a voice. I legally assist those on their journey of resiliency. Facing legal action, invoking rights, standing up for what you believe in, and seeking justice are all legal actions that require resilience. People are often intimidated by the legal system because it can be a complicated and costly experience when navigating it alone. The balancing act of emotions and decisions is imperative, and that is where I come in as their guide towards justice.

I took an oath to protect the rights of people and businesses to the fullest extent of the law. I made a personal oath to be a paralegal hero and a justice warrior. My clients see the passion and fire within me to educate, advise, mediate, and litigate. That comes from the ideas that have been formulated over years of facing obstacles and never giving up.

Being resilient for others is having the ability to put myself in the shoes of those that need a warrior to stand up and fight for their best interests. Every client and every case is different, but what remains the same is the consistency of mindset, persistence, and patience.

That is why I am who I am: Samantha F. Glass, the Owner and Managing Partner of **SFG Paralegal Services LLP**.

I took the passion I have within myself to face all my fears and all naysayers! I made a decision years ago that I wouldn't allow my desires to dwindle away. I took my formless substance of an idea from oh so long ago and put it in the palm of my hands like an invisible orb and turned it into a reality. It continues to grow every day so that and one day, it will span across the miles so that eventually, I will be assisting even more businesses and people with their legal matters across Ontario.

*"Be the warrior you are within, and let it radiate to the world. Be YOU and NEVER GIVE UP, NEVER GIVE IN!" SFG*

# Chapter Twenty-Five

## *We Are Strong Together*

∞

## *Satie Sekhon*

*"Life is a struggle, but you're not alone."*
*—Unknown*

I'll never forget my first day in Canada; the clean air as I stepped off the plane, the electricity, cars, and beautiful scenery- it was breathtaking. Growing up in Guyana, South America, life was quite different. It was a struggle for my family and me to build our dreams. We had no running water or power, so we used a kerosene lamp to provide light. Until the age of 16, I barely received an education. There was a school in my home country, but because uniforms were so expensive, we weren't able to attend. My life changed for the better when I received an invitation from my older brother to join him in Toronto, Ontario. At the time, I was a teenager and had already met my now-husband. We fell in love when we were both young, so it was no question that when my family and I would move, he also had that dream.

My first year in Canada was a struggle to get caught up on the education the country had to offer. When I arrived, I didn't know how to read, write, or even spell my own name. My brother began to teach me that when people say, "hi," that you have to say, "Hi," back. It's the simple things that so many Canadians do on a day-to-day basis that I was learning to do for the first time. It was a whole new world for me, but I was excited. I entered high school at the Grade 9 level, where I sat at the back of the class to observe. It took time, but I eventually was able to learn what I needed to in order to succeed.

I went on to graduate from the Learning Enterprise University of Guelph, and I was able to work for cultural link immigration and the early years centre. Not only that, but I was proud when I was able to get my driver's licence because it allowed me to have independence. My first job was working as Nanny alongside my mom. I have a certified childcare certificate from Mothercraft Institute. Being a caregiver is very much a part of me. I have worked in Day Cares and have cared for my family members since I can remember. Today, I'm the proud mom of three children, one girl, and two boys. My husband and I have been married for over twenty-five years and have continued to grow stronger as a couple, even through the hardships.

My husband has always been my role model. His entrepreneurial mindset has led the way to start a successful business for our family. In school, he studied auto-body mechanics and he opened his own Auto Body Technician Shop in Rexdale. As we grew, we were able to expand our horizons by purchases, not one, but two homes. We moved to Orangeville to a beautiful home just off Highway 10 and Beech Grove. It was 12-plus acre property, five bedrooms, four bathrooms, a dream home.

As the business grew, we had 23 flatbeds and tow trucks on the road, and my husband's opportunities were endless. We ended up moving to another home closer to the shop, so my husband didn't have to drive far distances during the night. We were happy about moving into our new home when the unexpected happened. In October 2015, there was a huge car pileup on Highway 401 in Whitby, and my son was the one who got hit with a tractor-trailer. My husband called me and said, "our son was in a car accident." He knew because he was called because the tow truck company was notified. I was beyond frantic as my husband hopped in his truck towards the scene to find my son. When he arrived, he was not able to locate my son because he was already on his way to the hospital. It is a miracle that he is alive, but my husband did not know that yet. He ran onto the 401, checking each car on the scene, the things he saw, and the suspense of not knowing where his son was would result in my husband suffering from post-traumatic stress disorder. He was traumatized.

My son suffered a major concussion, and we spent two years in and out of appointments to bring his memory back up to speed. Because of the trauma that my family endured, our lives and business took a turn. We were behind on our taxes and bills, and we were unable to pay our drivers. Everything we had was invested in the business, and because my husband wasn't able to hop on the highway like he used to, our business closed. It was a time in our lives that we didn't quite know how to climb our way out of, but eventually, we found hope.

Today, I'm a Financial Coach, and my husband is back on the road, driving a truck to sustain our lifestyle. My son is doing remarkable, and I'm so proud of him. We continue to grow together as a family unit, even though we live apart. My husband, my daughter, and I now live in Halifax, Nova Scotia, while my two boys (now grown), remain in Ontario. Each morning I wake up with a positive mindset, grateful that my family made it out of the chaos. We have worked our way out of debt, and I have so much joy every day as I get to help other families with their finances to get them out of debt.

I once heard someone say, "life is a struggle, but you are not alone." And that is so unbelievably true. The aftermath of our family trauma was tough, but together, we stayed resilient. Together, we are strong! - Satie

# Chapter Twenty-Six

## *How Resiliency Showed Me The Right Path*

⤲∞⤳

### *Carl Carty*

We all come from varied backgrounds, upbringing, and before you know it, you are an adult. I was in my early 20s, as a young man, trying to figure out where I wanted to go, who I wanted to be, and who I did not want to be. My faith was very strong as I looked to my Grandmother, God, and my step-mom. It was these women and God who grounded me. In life you have choices, I grew up with many people who made bad choices, too much partying, too much womanizing, no ambition, and they had children before they could take care of themselves. I knew this is not what I wanted.

I focused on helping my family and staying on the right path. I had three other siblings, including my younger brother, nine years younger than me. My mom worked shift work, and I saw her and my grandmother give up so much to support their family. They gave me such strong values. The Church and God were my sanctuaries. I went to school every day, worked part-time in the evenings, and helped my family as soon as I got home. By the age of 16, I started working part-time as a baker, took care of my younger brother, and knew I did not want to turn out like many of my friends or people I knew that had made bad choices.

By the time I was 21, I worked in a career that allowed me to make more money than most at that age, and I was just starting out. I started dating my wife, Michelle, and I knew I wanted more for us. My job paid me a lot of money, yet I wanted to increase my responsibility. I had a vision of becoming a crane operator and at that time, I was a welder and small machine operator. It became apparent to me after a couple of years as much as I would want to get the promotion, the bigger machine to drive, the company would give the role to a family member, even though many did not have the same experience or training. I remember one-day learning that I had a new supervisor. He could not speak any English and was brand new to Canada. He also never worked in the industry. Yet, he was my Supervisor. That notion took a toll on my mindset, yet at the same time I took a closer look at many people that stayed in this industry, and when I look now, some are not even alive, many aged, way beyond my years, so as a young adult I decided I wanted more.

I was scared to leave the type of money I was making. However, I knew I could take on more, and I believed in myself; I could do better; I knew there was something out there better for me; I was a man never to give up. The year my wife and I got married, I decided to leave my career to go back to school. Even this presented a few hiccups as my wife got laid off, and both of us weren't working. So, I stopped school for a year, found full-time work, then reapplied the following year. After I graduated, I was on my way towards my new path, and I was ready!

It was not easy; we did not have the internet; it was old fashion door knocking and speaking to everyone I knew to let them know I was looking for work. After a long seven month search, I finally secured a position. My wife was now working in Hamilton, Ontario, and we had been married almost nine years, living in Burlington, Ontario. We were secure and it was time for us to think about extending our family. Nine years is a long time to wait to have children when we both knew we wanted to be parents, however, we wanted to make sure we were secure as a couple before bringing children into the picture.

I look back now as a father of three beautiful daughters, my wife, my career, my relationship with my family, friends, and colleagues. I am who I am today because of my choices, I want people to know things may not always go the way you expect, life can be trying and challenging, life can be incredible, beautiful, and amazing. It's what we make of it. Today we live in a quiet, nice neighbourhood. I feel very blessed, yet I also want people to know it is not about the material things that make us who we are, it is the values that root us. I've always kept my faith in God, my Grandmother, my Mom, who both are in heaven today. All in my heart. You see, no matter who we are or where we came from, you and only you have free will to make a choice.

Today I have a beautiful life, I've watched my girls grow into strong intelligent beautiful young women Jovi, Jeanelle, and Serene. I am so blessed and so proud. I know when I reflect back, life could have gone in a different direction and my faith is what has kept me grounded. I truly hope my story inspires you when things are not going the way you want them to, dig deeper into your faith and belief. Just know there are better things waiting for you on the horizon.

If I were to offer any advice to any young person growing up today it would be to never give up, always follow your path, and always believe there is something out there better for you!

# Chapter Twenty-Seven

## Through Grief

❧

### Marcelle Wynter

May 8, 2009, I lost half my heart when I arrived home from work and found my 19-year-old son unconscious hanging from exercise equipment. He was a 6'5, lean, and muscular, and I knew that I would not have been able to get him down without assistance. I ran across the street to my friend, begging for help. I prayed to God to save him while feeling enormous guilt for wanting to save his life, obviously against his will.

My life changed forever that day. I struggled to make sense of what had happened and to find out why he thought ending his life was the answer. I wondered if I sheltered him too much, did I love him too much, did I do enough, or did I do too much? My heart broke just thinking that he was in so much pain, and he suffered alone. He used to ask me about world issues and why society viewed one race over another.

As my son got older, he became aware of societal prejudices and injustices. He was curious why certain races were hated and why individuals who commit blue-collar crimes were punished severely compared to white-collar crimes. He asked questions that were very political in regards to how society, individuals, and governments at the top deliberated actions to penalize and keep specific people in society paralyzed and marginalized. It was so difficult to answer these questions, but I always tried to be honest.

Grief squeezes your heart so hard that you can barely breathe, and the physical pain hurts so much that you feel as if you are having a heart attack. Your mind refuses to accept what you saw, refuses to believe that he is never coming home. What I have discovered about grief is that everyone has advice for you. I had another child to care for, and she was told by a coworker that I would never be the same. She was 17-years-old, and she was in pain, and she was so worried about me. I had to pull it together. I returned to work after a week, and I was just in a daze. I tried for a year to find answers regarding why he felt so hopeless that he thought his only option was to take his own life. It broke me apart. I realized that between guilt and sadness, I was never going to find the answers.

You find out who your friends are when you go through something like this. I lost a friend who I assume could not handle the sadness. People don't know how to speak with you or how to treat you, and sometimes they say hurtful things because they are not thinking, and they don't know what to say. I also found that there are wonderful people out there. My neighbours rallied around me and treated me like family. The children of the neighbourhood surprised me with their kindness and love. Children are so pure and honest, they say whatever comes to mind, and I have always loved them because of that.

We had a service of sorts at the funeral home, although I had spoken to both my children about what they would want us to do if they died. My son did not want a funeral where people just stared at this body, and although I wanted to adhere to his wish, I had to think about family and friends who would have wanted to say goodbye. We have the visitation and the funeral all within a couple of hours, and that is a day that I will never forget, although bits and pieces of it are lost to me.

The priest who preceded the service was amazing, and I say that from someone who is not religious. We went to visit him to work out the details of the service at his residence in the church. He had a beautiful black lab. The dog looked at everyone in the room, and she came next to me. This beautiful animal then rested her head on my knee and proceeded to pull herself up, and she put both her front paws around my neck. I remember sobbing into the neck of this beautiful dog as if my life was over, and in some respects, a part of me died that I can never get back.

We had to meet with the people at the funeral home, and I remember how completely out of it I was. I could not wrap my mind around the fact that he was gone and never coming home. They led us to one coffin after another and showed up various urns. I think that the funeral home business should be changed because these salespeople are taking advantage of grief-stricken families when they are at their worst and try to convince them to purchase things that they don't need. I was told that I should go to group counselling and so many things were thrown at me. I arranged for my daughter to get counselling and then I thought about what I needed. I realized that group therapy would not work for me because I was already sad; I did not want to be in a room full of other people who were also in pain.

I ended up seeing a bereavement counsellor, which helped me to get through the minutes, hours, and days of grief. We need to understand that everyone grieves in their own way. I did not grieve in public, I cried as I walked, and I cried at home alone. This seemed to surprise and offend some people. I was even challenged by a doctor who was concerned that I was not showing signs of grief at work and that surprised me. I asked him if his employer would continue to pay him if he came to work, and cried every day. I told him that I grieved in my own time and in my own way and that I did not need to take the medication that I was being prescribed because I did not want to be numb to the pain as I had heard others describe. I wanted to feel my way through it.

We need to find out what each person needs, don't assume that they need things, ask. If you don't know what to say, just ask if there is anything that you can do or if that person needs anything. Drop off food for them and respect their privacy but always reach out and keep in touch. When you are alone, and the funeral is over, and all the family and friends are gone, that is when grief comes in full force. If you have lost a child or anyone you love, please remember the good times. If you are someone contemplating suicide or self-harm, please know that you are loved and that someone cares and that you matter and that you are enough!

Our medical system is not working for people with mental health issues. If you are lucky enough to have additional benefits through your workplace, the amount allotted to counselling is alarming. If you have been given medication, you are left on your own without follow up care. If someone is lost and feeling alone and thinking of self-harm, giving medication without follow-up is detrimental to them. We need to treat mental illness for what it is, a medical condition. Whether your mental illness is a chemical imbalance or induced by trauma, people need care and should not be ostracized. Mental illness is something that some people struggle with all their lives. We need to help, and we need to do so now before we lose more people. Their lives matter!

My son was such a beautiful young man. Today is the 11<sup>th</sup> anniversary of his death. I focus every year on celebrating his birthday because I feel that I was so blessed to have him in my life for 19 years.

Through grief, I found resiliency, and my son lives on through my heart every day.

# Chapter Twenty-Eight

## *Resilient for My Clients*

Ↄ∞ↄ

## *Cindy Zupanoovic*

My name is Cindy Zupanovic, and as a Realtor, Resiliency is my life. I would like to share a unique story highlighting the resiliency of trust, working with new clients navigating them through the process of securing their very first million-dollar investment opportunity.

I met Patti and Ian, a couple who had never purchased a 2nd property for investment. They had some knowledge and knew they wanted a multi-income property, a house with a duplex status. They knew how to calculate the numbers and what their bottom line was. They knew the building (or what we call total combined income, the collected rent) had to bring in enough money to satisfy the mortgage, the taxes and insurance plus potentially have cash flow. Their initial thoughts were let's find a home we can reno and turn into a duplex, this would be the start.

Patti and Ian had no idea on the process, what or where to buy, how to assess the condition, how to weigh the risks, the landscape and competitiveness of the market. This is where I came in to assess their major needs and desires and to what level their handiness was, as they were about to onboard hundreds of thousands of dollars of debt. As a Real Estate Investor myself, we call this GOOD Debt. You see when you borrow lenders money at low interest (not yours), and you can provide affordable living for people who need this, you are helping everyone and this is why I serve. Oh, I forgot to mention my clients were also about to become landlords, a brand new role they have never taken on.

Once I gained a solid understanding of where they were and the initial budget of what they wanted to spend, we got the search started. Ian and Patti had a smaller budget in mind, they thought if they found a property they could reno, the costs would be lower and the outcome would be the same. After viewing options they learned it would be a challenge, in construction and legal apartments, there are many other factors, zoning, permits, legal vs non-legal, implications, so it's really like being a real estate solution consultant with a legal background. My role was not to just find a place, as an investor myself, I knew the numbers had to work and so many variables had to be considered to protect my clients and the risks. The market was hot and we experienced bidding wars, Ian and Patti soon realized pricing is a strategy, they had to revisit their original budget and they had to react fast. I decided to introduce them to another investor friend client I have. This client was able to share insight as he came from experience. Patti and Ian found this comforting, as anyone who is going through this type of a big decision, Resiliency it the #1 trait we all need to have to reach across the finish line. To see my clients happy with their new investment property is the goal. It has to be a win-win scenario. Purchasing real estate whether for personal or investment it is not a transaction, this is an end to end process, conception to completion.

After Patti and Ian spent some time with me, my client and investor friend, they really started to understand the costs, and had to look at this differently, they increased their budget and started to look at duplex and triplex that were already built. They realized if they spend less on the reno trying to do the complete transformation of taking a home and converting it, they could take this reno cost and add to their budget and look for an existing duplex or triplex. I work in partnership with my clients, every client has different needs and it is not a cookie-cutter approach. The beginning of the journey with Ian and Patti allowed for them to see and learn, they soon realized how intense the project would be to get the job done, getting the permits, hiring the crew as one person could not work fast enough on their own. It became more clear why you need a team lead led by an experienced realtor professional who understands the impact of these costs.

When Ian and Patti made this decision, they budgeted approximately eight months to carry before all units would be rented, they were hoping to have one floor or one unit rented when they purchased and it became apparent they had to look at this investment differently. If they increased their budget, reduced the reno time and cost, look for a more ready legal duplex that would give them the results they were looking for. If I had taken this approach with my clients in the beginning my clients would never have experienced the why.

During the beginning with their original plan and budget, we did end up putting a couple of offers on properties yet during my due diligence we uncovered the units may not be legal, one property we walked away from after we did the inspection, the property looked amazing and post-inspection changed everything, too much risk. It was after they spent some time learning the process with me and speaking with my investor client, they came to the conclusion and realized the heavy risks involved if you purchase a property with a non-conforming legal unit.

After having dinner one night with Patti and Ian, they agreed to increase their budget and start looking at existing duplexes and triplexes. Shortly thereafter we found the perfect property. It was a bidding war however by this time we were a solid team and knew how to win.

Today, Patti and Ian are thrilled. The resilience it took to accomplish this was by far one of the most rewarding and to see the happiness on my client's faces, nothing beats this feeling. When you are leading and you are responsible for not just the purchase, the risks that can apply, both on behalf of my client Patti and Ian and myself, it takes an enormous amount of trust to have this type of relationship. I adore Patti and Ian and am so blessed to have represented them and have them as clients for life.

In closing, I would like to thank my Father in spirit with us today. I could write an entire book however I want to leave you all with how important it is when you have passion to act. My dad was my role model, he took risks when we were young, he purchased commercial buildings, became a landlord while working full time doing shift work in a different industry. He was not a realtor yet he was a businessman and knew how money worked. I learned more from my Dad and value his gifts he taught me. I know he is with me every day. Real Estate is the best investment anyone could ever make, you need a trusted team and always believe there is a solution.

# Chapter Twenty-Nine

## Life Redesign

❦

### Rosetta Qadhi

I was born in a rural part of Jamaica with almost zero access to basic amenities and social infrastructure. I'm the sixth of the seven children in my family, and I spent most of my life away from my immediate family's warmth. I never got to enjoy unity or even understood why I was here.

The poverty within our family circle was constant and overwhelming. I remember the days when I was so hungry and weak, all I could do was lay in bed. In the early year of 1989, the financial circumstances got to be too much for my parents, so they sent me to live with my aunt, which was the beginning of a very long journey within my family circle.

Throughout my childhood, I was passed around from one relative to another, feeling as though I was an unwanted object that nobody wanted to keep for too long. As a young child, I couldn't understand why. I always obeyed the rules. I was kind and caring, but yet no one wanted me to stay with them. At some point, I thought that there was something wrong with me.

Eventually, I ended up alone in a boarding school. But, in all, I became my own mother and father. I learned how to love and take care of myself. Being alone made me strong. It made me tough and gave me the power of resilience.

At a very young age, I knew that if I wanted a better life, I would have to do it myself. In the summer of 1991, one morning after a long night of tossing and turning, I woke up with many thoughts, visualization, and introspection. That morning, that year, I started to design the life I wanted to have.

For many of us, our life journeys and experiences make us do the things we do. For some, it just happened. For me, it was both. I told myself I can never be behind the stage and remain unknown. I knew the huge task ahead, but I was willing to pay the price. I had visualized my entire life like a movie and set out a blueprint, but I had only God to see me through.

Today, I am a successful businesswoman, who defied the odds growing up; taking it upon myself to change my circumstances through the power of MY MIND. I created my life's blueprint in my mind and took the steps I needed to design the life I imagined down into reality. My success has grown with each step I take. I am now helping people around the world change their lives for the better, reaching their goals through the power of their minds. I write to let you know that with every achievement brings new challenges. New levels bring new challenges, but the power of YOUR MIND can help make it an easier ride.

So, how did I get from being a poor broke girl to a successful woman?

Well, I must thank my parents because if they didn't send me away, I wouldn't be who I am today. They did what they thought would be best for me. I could've easily blamed them and played the role of a victim, which wouldn't help me at all in this world, instead, I used my abandonment, my rejections as a fuel to propel me forward.

So, how did I get to where I am?

NUMBER ONE: PRIORITIZE WHAT I WANTED AND I ELIMINATED THE UNNECESSARY. I didn't spend time with anything or anyone that kept my agenda at bay. I refuse to give unnecessary things my time and energy.

NUMBER TWO: I WENT WITHIN FOR MY ANSWERS. As I began to create my life, I realized that it was important for me to listen to my own inner guidance. Often, we sit around waiting for others to tell us what to do or where to go, and we don't end up not doing anything nor go anywhere at all. Or we take their advice, and we end up going down the wrong path. I never sat around waiting and hoping for something good to happen to me. Whatever I wanted, I went after it. I'm giving you the same advice, don't spend your time waiting and hoping for a saviour. Do not sit around waiting for a sign; the sign is within you; all you have to do is stop and look at it.

NUMBER THREE: I KEPT MY GOD CLOSE TO ME. I knew that there were going to be attributes of my walk, of my design that was going to be different from others, and it would require me to have a close relationship with my God. With the faith and the trust that I have in my God and in myself, I know that I can make the impossible possible.

So I tell you today your relationship with your God, must be so close that his lips must be resting on your ears because some of the things that he will direct some of you to create will be so far out there that those around you will say; no! They'll tell you that you're wrong; they'll tell you that you can't; they'll call you crazy, and if you believe them, you're going to miss God. You'll also miss all the beautiful opportunities that are in front of you, and those that are coming towards you.

NUMBER FOUR: I OVERCAME MY FEARS. I had to track down my fears and my desires. I dealt with my fears head-on. Then I positioned myself to go after the things I so strongly desired because my desire for success was stronger than my fears of failing.

NUMBER FIVE: I WAS PERSISTENT. I knew that in order to get to where I wanted to go, I was going to have to have the discipline to persist because no matter what we want to create, there will be roadblocks and barriers along the way as soon as I made a commitment. Why? Because it is a part of the automatic function of the mind. Whenever you decide to create something new, everything that was previously created that is in conflict with that new thing rises up and re-assert itself. This is the cause of many failures than anything else.

Once you begin to follow these steps, you'll not only begin to redesign your life; you'll become resilient too!

# Chapter Thirty

## *Giving Back*

❧

### *Gloria Duguay*

My life began on November 30th, 1941 in Hastings, Ontario, a small town east of Peterborough. I was the firstborn in my family which expanded to become a family of seven children. My earliest memory as a child is when I was about five years old when my father got a job in a gold mine in a community called Central Patricia in Northern Ontario. By this time, my family had grown to include a brother and sister.

My father went on his way and my mother later brought me and my siblings to Toronto where we got on a train to Sioux Lookout, Ontario. Since there were no roads into the community, we had to travel the rest of the way by plane. I remember being so sick on the way there that I threw up in a paper bag and when we arrived, there was so much snow on the ground.

My memory was fuzzy from that point on until we moved back to Southern Ontario and moved in with my Aunt and Uncle who owned a dairy farm. Their family included eight children. We were cousins growing up with one another and became one big happy family. To this day we are all still remarkably close.

Living on the farm with my cousins was a lot of fun. We all went to school in a little one-room schoolhouse with no indoor plumbing, no running water, and no central heating. The school was heated with a potbelly wood burning stove and we had one teacher for all of us, made up of about 50 children from grades 1 to 8.

After living with my Aunt and Uncle for about a year and a half, my father bought a little two-room house about a mile from my Uncle's farm. I was probably about ten years old at that time. Like our school, we had no running water, no indoor plumbing, and no electricity. We were poor, but did we know we were poor? No but it did not take long before I discovered why.

Eventually, I learned that my father suffered from an addiction. Unlike most people who have addictions to things like drugs, alcohol, etc; my father's addiction was to cars. He just could not pass a used car lot without going in and he would more times than not, leave with a different car than the one he drove in. His behaviour resulted in having a revolving loan payment. Therefore, there was not a lot of money for food nor any other necessities of life.

My father was also shiftless. He had no problem finding employment. He just could not hold down a steady job. The lack of money when I was growing up caused a lot of tension and fighting between my parents. It also left me with a lot of emotional scarring. I went on to high school in Belleville in 1954 at the age of 12, turning 13 in November and having skipped a grade. Going from a small one room school with around 35 to 40 students to an exceptionally large school in the city with a student population of around 1500 to 1600 students was a huge culture shock for me, but I made a promise to myself that I would graduate, get a job, and never live in poverty again.

I graduated from grade twelve in 1958 and started my very first job at the age of 16, three days after finishing school in June, at a salary of $35.00 a week. I thought I was a millionaire. I remember my first purchase was a pair of red high heel shoes. I wore them out of the store and never having walked in heels before, I ended up with a few blisters.

After a few years, I changed jobs and went to work in a large telecom company where I met the man who would become my husband. We were married a year after we met. Two years later, the telecom company was expanding with the building of a plant in a new community outside the City of Toronto and offered transfers to employees who expressed their wish to relocate. My husband was one of those employees. I was nervous about leaving my family, but at the same time, I was extremely excited.

I was embarking on a new chapter in my life and moving into a brand-new home in a new city where I knew no one. All of the excitement and being a young mother with two little boys was not enough to keep me from becoming extremely homesick. I would call my mom several times a week and finally, her advice to me was "Gloria, get a job!" I applied to the telecom company and was hired almost immediately. Fortunately, there was a nursery school in our community where I enrolled the boys and they both loved their new environment.

I began to become more settled as winter was approaching. With the coming of winter also brought winter activities such as minor hockey. My husband was an avid sports fan and he thought it would be a good idea to put our oldest son in hockey. Eventually, both boys were playing hockey and my husband decided he would coach minor hockey. He did not coach our boys; he chose to coach older boys who played rep hockey. This meant travelling to other centres.

Our family grew to four children with the addition of two little girls. With the boys playing hockey, my husband coaching and travelling, meant he was away from home a lot leaving me home alone with the kids which left me very lonely and somewhat depressed. To combat both my depression and loneliness, I decided also to get involved in the community. I enrolled our girls in activities, and I joined several organizations, which made me discover that giving back to the community not only brought me so much joy and gratitude, but I no longer felt lonely when my husband was out also giving back to the community.

Over the years, times changed as our children grew up, got married, and moved away. Both my husband and my parents passed, but I continue to stay resilient with my approach to life. Through keeping busy and giving back to others when possible, I allow myself to enjoy life.

# Chapter Thirty-One

## *Our First Business*

⚬⚭⚬

### *Roy Cleeves*

The year was 1998, and we were very excited about opening our first business—a Jumbo Video store. We thought that it would be a lot of fun because we really love movies, so we decided to do this as our business.

As the first year rolled on, the business made a profit, and then as things started to change for the second year, we barely broke even. By our third year, our top clients were now streaming videos and using satellite dish receivers. It became very clear that we could not survive financially to keep the business open. So, we decided to seek the advice of a trustee and put our business into receivership.

The receiver suggested that we make a consumer proposal and payout everyone we could from the business on a schedule. This was a good plan and very fair, and it was all in progress until the trustee made it clear that we would have to give up all of our credit cards and live only on a cash basis. This created a gut reaction in my wife, and she started to cry as she could not envision living only on a cash basis. I began to think that we had made a major mistake as it seemed to be the end of good living for us. My feelings led me to ask the receiver, what else could we do? The receiver said all we could do is our own private proposal because we only had four secured creditors and maybe a dozen unsecured creditors.

Our strategy worked exactly the same as a consumer proposal, except I was the one in control. I was the one choosing what I would be able to payout to the various creditors. The plan would also keep it away from the Credit Bureau, and therefore we could keep our credit cards and our credit standing in good shape. Our secured creditors immediately agreed.

By 2001, we were on to our new lives as we moved back closer to the hometown where our family was close for support. During our time of settling our debts and starting over, it became stressful, and with that stress, you begin to question your relationship. I often thought— would my wife still want to be with me knowing that I had failed at this business? There was no doubt as she reminded me that we did the business together, and it wasn't my failure alone and also that the market had changed, and people began to stream videos instead of renting them. Her support made me feel really good and made me commit that whatever became my next career, I was going to do so well and ensure that we built up a big bank of funds that we would not have to worry about ever being in this position again.

It wasn't long before I decided that real estate would be my new career. My decision was going to be a bigger risk because of the fact that real estate pays commission only, and there is no salary when you're starting out. I knew that I would have to sell one house a month to be able to continue to cover our living expenses, and if I wanted to progress our family, I would have to sell at least one more house a month. Just like any business, it would take a lot of work and a lot of energy, but I was inspired to do just that!

I began to do open houses every weekend and advertised homes for sale on a regular basis. I also took every call on the first ring. Soon, I was so busy selling homes that I needed help. I decided that the best person for the job would be my wife, Nikki. Choosing Nikki would also allow us to keep most of our money in my family.

I taught Nikki exactly how to search for homes for my clients and how to email them directly with a personal note saying, "I think this one looks good and I think we should consider it. Please let me know when you'd like to go and see it." My clients would call me up and say, "Roy, I want to go see that one," and I would have to literally ask them which one it was since I really didn't know because I was so busy.

In my first full year, I sold 60 homes, and in my second full year, I sold 98 homes. I realized my new career was an incredible turn of fortune. I was well on my way to making sure that I could build up the reserves that I wanted to make sure that I would never be in that position again, where my wife would be crying about not having enough money.

It was at the age of 40-years-old when I started my new career. I can truly advise you that you are never too old to have a career in real estate as the clients appreciate the fact that you have some life experience and can talk about that when you talk with them about buying or selling the home. My career in real estate led to the best two decades so far in my life!

We were able to bounce back from the brink of bankruptcy to now hold millions of dollars in real estate and become Millionaires!

My advice to you is that you are never too old to start something new. Everyone is capable of taking something you are passionate about and turning it into a very profitable business! So, if things are not going the way you want them to in your present career, put on a brave face and start a new career today!

# Conclusion

As you turn the final page of our book, we hope you leave us feeling encouraged to practice resilience in your life today. May these stories stick with you to uplift your energy in times of need and motivate you to write your own resiliency story one day! The Resiliency team thanks all of you for reading our *30 + 1 Stories.*

# Editor

The developmental editing for *30+1 Resilient Stories* was created by Linsey Fischer.

Linsey is an Editor, Writing Coach, and Ghostwriter. She has coached over one-hundred aspiring authors to share their message through writing and has won an award for the work she did on the *Empowering Women* book series.

Check for updates from our editor, author(s), and team for upcoming projects and collaborations.

Thank you for taking this journey with us!